A Scripture Union resource book

ULTIMATE
Games

Patrick Goodland

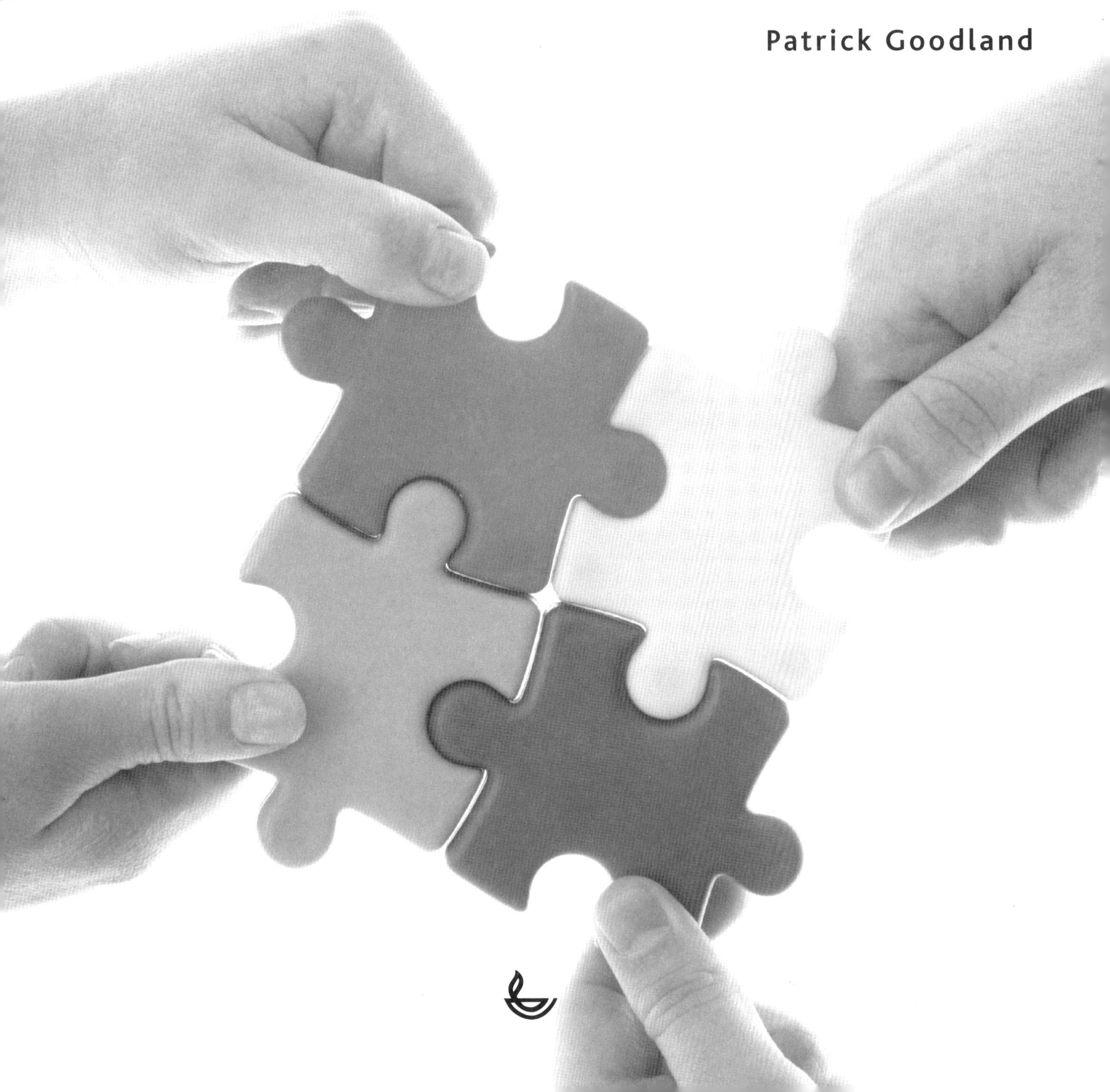

© Patrick Goodland 1979 Over 300 Games

This edition Ultimate Games published 2008
ISBN 978 1 84427 365 2

Scripture Union, 207–209 Queensway, Bletchley, MK2 2EB, England.
Email: info@scriptureunion.org.uk
Website: www.scriptureunion.org.uk

Scripture Union Australia, Locked Bag 2, Central Coast Business Centre, NSW 2252 Australia
Website: www.scriptureunion.org.au

Scripture Union USA, PO Box 987, Valley Forge, PA 19482, USA
Website: www.scriptureunion.org

All rights reserved. No part of this publication may be reproduced, stored in a retrieval system, or transmitted, in any form or by any means, electronic, mechanical, photocopying, recording or otherwise, without the prior permission of Scripture Union.

The right of Patrick Goodland to be identified as author of this work has been asserted by him in accordance with the Copyright, Designs and Patents Act 1988.

British Library Cataloguing-in-Publication Data
A catalogue record for this book is available from the British Library.
Printed and bound in Singapore by Tien Wah Press Ltd
Cover design by Wild Associates
Internal layout by C Michael Lorenz

Scripture Union is an international Christian charity working with churches in more than 130 countries, providing resources to bring the good news about Jesus to children, young people and families and encouraging them to develop spiritually through the Bible and prayer.

As well as our network of volunteers, staff and associates who run holidays, church-based events and school Christian groups, we produce a wide range of publications and support those who use our resources through training programmes.

ULTIMATE
Games

Introduction

Games are for physical relaxation and real enjoyment. They help us to share fun, make friends and break down reserve and shyness. They are, in short, communication tools. This is a practical handbook for all who are involved in activities with children, young people and families. All the games have been tried with success. Many of their origins are unknown and some will be recognised as variations on well-known themes.

- Careful preparation, the sharing of responsibility, and having a varied programme are three of the secrets of success.

- A great number of the games may be adapted to suit the number of participants, their age group and the local conditions. When choosing games, it is important to think carefully about the players and the situation. For example, some teenagers will enjoy pencil and paper games but others may be embarrassed by them. Don't embarrass 'winners' or 'losers', or anyone who is disabled. Be flexible and caring.

- When leading games, it is essential to understand the rules yourself and to explain them clearly and briefly. It is often possible to begin the game and teach the rules as the game develops. With larger groups, using a microphone will help to keep control and ensure that the rules are clearly heard and understood.

- Rules and regulations should be upheld to the degree necessary for discipline and enjoyment, but remember that over-enthusiastic referees can cause endless irritation and rob games of their fun.

- Where a game needs items of equipment, this is stated in italics before each game is explained. The equipment should be collected in advance. Don't, for example, ask for scarves to make blindfolds in the middle of a programme. Sometimes people who can't or won't join in a game can be given responsibility and tasks such as looking after the equipment or keeping score.

- Timing is an important factor; so is the choice of your opening game which you may have to play when only a handful of the players have arrived.

- Change games while they are still successful. Don't wait until they have been played too long and interest is flagging.

- Take account of weather conditions. Don't allow children to stand around on cold, windy days and don't overtax them in a heat wave. If they are playing lots of energetic games, particularly in the summer, you may also want to provide them with cold drinks.

- Adults should never monopolise a game for younger players, but a little encouragement for the losing team, especially in field games, will often renew enthusiasm. Players need encouragement and affirmation.

- Safety is important. Choose your games responsibly and play with adequate supervision.

- Be enthusiastic at all times – it's infectious!

Acknowledgements

I would like to thank Pip Wilson for permission to use 'Lace up' and 'Balloon Shavers' from his book, *Games without Frontiers*, published by HarperCollins. I extend similar thanks to Scripture Union for permission to use some of their ideas on parachute games and the canopy storytelling by Michael Wells on page 24.

Contents

Section 1	Outdoor games for groups	7
Section 2	Parachute games	22
Section 3	Sports day ideas	26
Section 4	Indoor games for the very young	29
Section 5	Games for Junior children (6 to 11s)	34
Section 6	Indoor games for young people	54
Section 7	Games with balloons	72
Section 8	Paper and pencil games	76
Section 9	Party fun and entertainment	86
Section 10	Travel games	93

Key

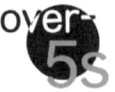

over-5s	= for over 5s age group
over-8s	= for over 8s age group
over-11s	= for over 11s age group
over-15s	= for over 15s age group
all-age	= all ages
more than 15	= more than 15 players required
lots of space	= plenty of space required
messy	= a messy game
team game	= team game

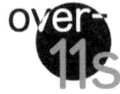

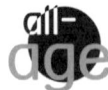

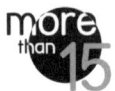

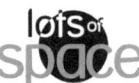

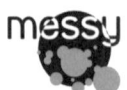

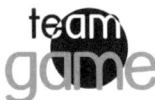

ULTIMATE Games

1 Outdoor games for groups

1 Adapted hockey

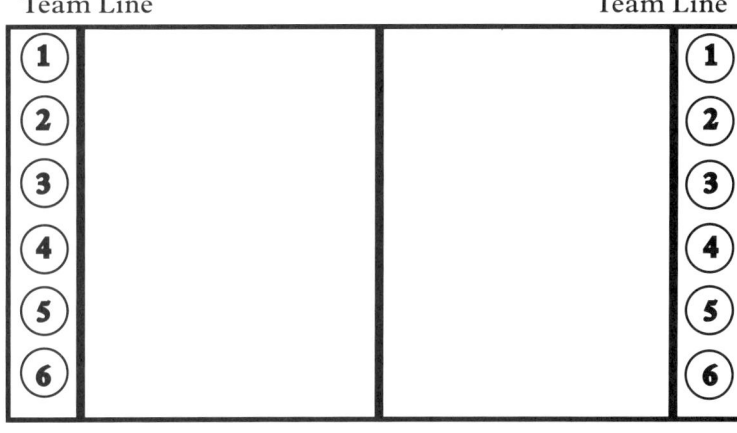

You will need:

A shinty or hockey stick for each player
A frido ball (a vinyl ball, about 220 mm diameter)
Masking tape, paint, rope or chalk to mark the team lines

Set a time limit in which to play the game (this will depend on the stamina and enthusiasm of the players). The pitch should be roughly the size of a tennis court. Five or six players in each team is best, but a few more or less makes no difference. You will also need to appoint someone to be the referee. The aim of the game is to score goals. The winning team is the one with the most goals at the end of the time of play.

Divide the players into two teams, and line the teams up behind two lines on each side of the pitch, facing each other. Number the players on each team 1–6 (or higher depending on the number of players). The referee rolls the ball into the middle, between the two teams, and calls out a number. The two players with that number run forward and try to get the ball over their opponents' line, using their shinty sticks. The other players attempt to prevent this from happening by defending their lines with their sticks. However, defending team members are not allowed to go over their team lines, and none of the players may lift his stick above his shoulder or kick the ball deliberately. As soon as the ball crosses the line a goal is scored; the referee then collects the ball, rolls it into the middle, calls out another number, and the game begins again.

2 Back-to-back battle

over-5s

You will need:

Masking tape, paint, rope or chalk to mark the team lines
A time limit for each round of this team contest is essential

Mark two parallel lines on the floor, approximately 7 m apart. Divide the players into two teams. Two players from each team stand back to back, midway between the two lines. On the word 'Go', each player pushes backwards in an attempt to push the other across her team line.

3 Balloon-bag burst

over-8s messy

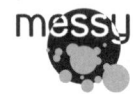

You will need:

A balloon filled with water
A long sock for each player

This is a variation on tag games. Players should be of similar age and stature.

The players are each given a water balloon which they insert into their socks. The object of the game is for each player to hit and burst another's balloon while protecting her own. Hitting must always be from the shoulder down. Whenever someone's balloon bursts, she is 'out' of the game.

4 Banana duel

over-8s messy

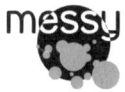

You will need:

Lots of ripe bananas

Two players stand back to back, each with a banana in his pocket. On the referee's command, 'Let the duel begin', the players try to peel the banana with one hand only. Biting off the end of the banana is not allowed. The first to succeed then turns round and squashes it in the other player's face.

Beware of messy clothing. This game is great fun!

5 Big-bag ball escape

over-8s more than 15 team game

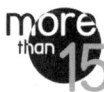

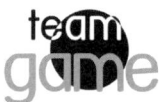

You will need:

A bin-bag
Some balloons

To prepare for the game, blow the balloons up and put them in the bin-bag. Tie the bag securely. Set a time limit for each round of the game.

Divide the players into two equally numbered teams, and ask everyone to take their shoes off. One team makes an outer circle around the other which forms an inner circle. Both teams lie on their backs, shoeless, with their heads pointing towards the centre. The big-bag ball is thrown into the centre. The inner team tries to kick or hit the ball over the heads of the outer team. Goals are scored when they succeed and the ball lands on the ground outside the circle. The inner team must stay lying down throughout the game. The outer team may use their hands and arms, but are not allowed to move their feet. The winning team is the one with the most goals scored by the end of the game session.

Make sure that both teams have the same amount of time in the inner circle. Fairly frequent changes ensure greater excitement.

6 Blast-off

This is a good seaside or field game, which can be played in groups of mixed ages. Work to a prepared script like those outlined below, which can be adapted to suit local conditions and the age of the participants. The background to Script 1 is a journey into space; Script 2 describes being marooned on a desert island. The groups act out each moment of the drama in a series of exercises. When one group has finished an exercise, they are awarded points before moving on to the next. A leader from each group reads out the instructions, and a referee is in charge of each team to ensure that they carry them out. Have a starting and finishing point for each group.

Script 1
- Before the spaceship can leave the starbase, each player must find a piece of wood.
- You are now in space, and the crew has become weightless. Collect six stones, each at least as big as your fist.
- It is time for your first meal. Collect some seaweed (a leaf) for each member of the crew.
- The ship is being invaded by aliens. Make a hole (find a space) big enough for all the crew to hide in.
- The captain has gone down with fever and needs water. Fetch him/her some water in a container of some kind, at least one cupful.
- All the crew under nine years of age have caught a mysterious disease. The rest of the crew (or the captain) must carry them at least 18 m.
- The spaceship lands on Mars, and the ground there is getting very hot. The captain wheelbarrows half the team to the landing area (the finishing point). The rest must collect three shells/pebbles each before they can follow him.
- When everyone has reached the landing area, dig for 'precious stones' (wrapped sweets or other prizes), one (or more) for each crew member.

Script 2
- Each member of the crew collects a twig and a leaf (a stick and scrap paper) to make a flag.
- Before setting sail, the crew need to collect enough stores: pebbles for meat; flowers (or shells) for dessert; leaves (or seaweed) for vegetables. The biggest pile gets bonus points.
- Half the crew are down with scurvy. Collect as many kinds of green leaf as you can.
- Pirates are sighted on the forward beam. Collect stones more than six inches in diameter, for cannon-balls. Each sailor should have three cannon-balls.
- The ship is sinking. Every sailor finds some 'driftwood' to cling to.
- Find 'an island' big enough for all the crew to stand in.
- The sun is getting very hot. Build 'a hut' to protect the smallest member of your crew.
- While exploring the island, you see that the pirates have landed and made a camp which is surrounded by a wall. Beyond the wall is a fire in the distance, with guards all around it. You need to get past the camp without being seen, before you can get to where you will be rescued. Advance cautiously for about 15 m, keeping your ears and eyes open.
- The pirates manage to wound all crew members over twelve years old. The wounded sailors must be helped towards the point of rescue (the finishing line).

7 Building a pyramid

You will need:

Several boxes of a similar size, each marked in the team colours
Team markers (eg cardboard circles weighted down with stones), each colour-marked according to the teams
A plank of wood, about 1.5 m long
A washing-line or rope at least 30 m long, to make a circle

Make a large circle with the rope. Place the markers at an equal distance around the perimeter. Place an equal number of boxes at each marker; each pile of boxes should be the same colour.

Divide the players into teams of three, and give each team a plank. The teams go to their allotted places (perhaps they could wear their team colours). Two team members are the 'slaves' who must carry the boxes, one by one, on the plank, moving from base to base around the circle. The third team member is the 'overseer'. All three team members must 'touch base', ie touch the markers, as they visit them. If a box falls off the plank at any time, only the overseer can put it back on – the slaves are not allowed to help. Each time a team gets back to home base, they use the boxes they have carried to build a pyramid.

Overtaking is allowed, except when a team is at a base. The teams cannot knock over each other's pyramids en route either. The winning team is the first to finish the course and complete the pyramid with all their boxes.

8 Capture the flag

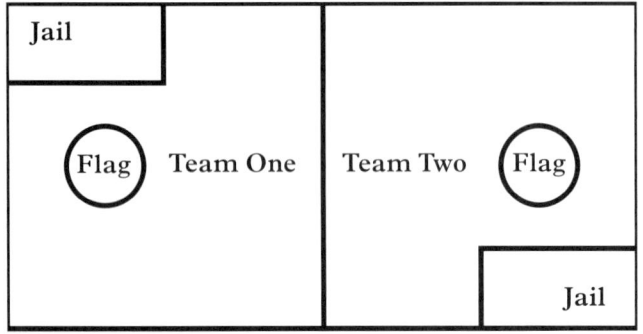

You will need:

Two small flags on poles
Masking tape, paint, rope or chalk to mark the field of play

This game is a 'golden oldie' which never seems to fade in its appeal both to players and spectators.

Mark out a large field of play (see diagram). Divide the players into two teams who take up any position on their side of the field. The purpose of the game is to capture the opposing team's flag without getting tagged. A team's flag is captured if a member of the other team manages to grab it and get it back to home territory without being caught. The home team chases and tries to tag any member of the opposing side who steps into their home territory. If players are caught, they are put in jail. If a team member can reach the jail of the opposing side without being tackled, he may tag his comrades and set them free. The freed prisoners have a free walk back to safety.

The success of this game depends on strategy, diversion, ingenuity, speed and good team-work. No other form of 'blocking' (eg holding, scrumming) other than tagging may be used.

9 Circle pass out

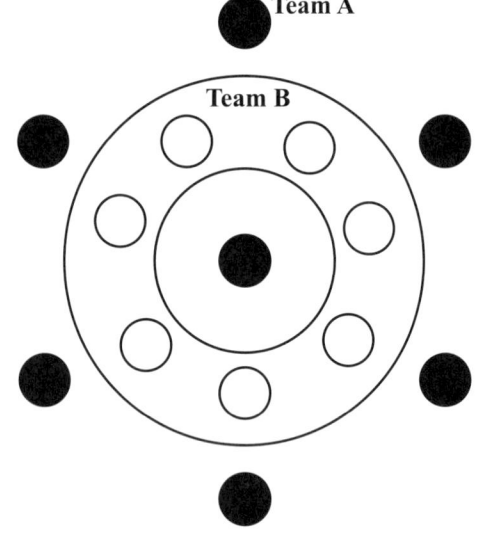

You will need:

A small ball
A large rubber ball or football
Chalk, to draw the circles

This is a fairly advanced circular passing and intercepting game. Set a time limit of, say, three or four minutes for each round.

Draw two large circles, and arrange the players as shown in the diagram. The centre player tries to throw the ball to the outside players, not going above shoulder height. The players between the two circles try to intercept the ball as it is thrown. A score is kept of the number of good passes.

After one round, the inside team changes places with the outside one, and the game is restarted. A new thrower takes the place of the original one. If the numbers are particularly large, two, three, or even four centre throwers could be introduced.

10 Collection relay

You will need:

Masking tape, paint, rope or chalk to mark the starting line and the crossing line

Mark the starting line and the crossing line, which run parallel to each other about 20m apart. Divide the players into equally numbered teams.

The first runner in a team runs from the starting line, over the crossing line, then runs back and grasps the hand of the second runner. They both run over the crossing line, then both go back to pick up the third runner. The three now run together over the course and go back to pick up the fourth runner, and so on until all six are over the crossing line. Play the game again, in the opposite direction, but this time the last runner of the previous round is the first to start the return journey. The race is complete when all the team are back to their original starting position.

11 Cops and robbers

No equipment needed

This game may be played as a single group or competitively between two teams.

Choose two people to be the cop and the robber. The rest of the players hold hands and form three or four lines: they are the streets and alleyways down which the cop must chase the robber. The chase begins, but on the command 'Change!', the 'streets and alleyways' make a quarter turn to the left or right and immediately link up again, to form new streets running in different directions. The cop and the robber have to adjust to the new street map. The unbreakable rule is that neither of the two can pass through the players' linked hands.

If there is no 'catch' within a set time limit, the role of the cop and the robber is taken by two other players, while the first two join in helping to make the streets and alleyways.

12 Crocker

You will need:

Three stumps to make a wicket
A large ball
A baseball bat or rounders stick

There are many variations and rules for this game, but the following have been among the best. The smaller the two teams are the better, though they should not be under ten players each.

Place the three stumps so that they form a wicket 1m wide. Put the bowler's stump 6m away in front of the wicket, and the runner's stump 6m or more away to the left of the wicket.

The bowler throws the ball from his stump, bowling underarm, full toss (ie the ball shouldn't touch the ground before the batsman can hit it) and aiming between the knee and the shoulder of the batsman. The batsman runs round the runner's stump every time he hits the ball in front of the wicket. The bowler can bowl again as soon as the ball returns to him.

The batsman may be bowled out (the ball hits the wicket) or be deemed out l.b.w. if the ball hits him twice. He may also be caught out full toss (someone catches the ball before it hits the ground) and if the ball is caught behind the wicket. To speed up the game, the whole team can be out when one of their team is caught full toss; or each player can be out if the ball bounces once before it is caught.

The winning team is the one with the most runs after a set number of innings.

13 Dodge ball

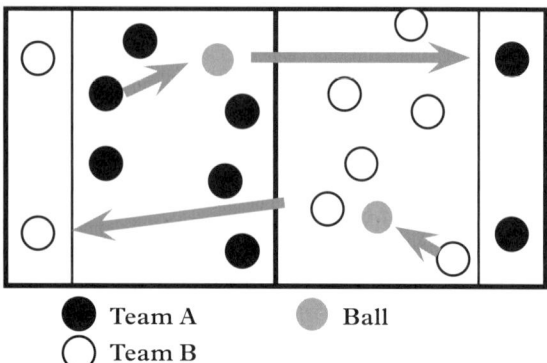

● Team A ● Ball
○ Team B

You will need:

Two or more soft balls, depending on age, skill and number of players
Masking tape, paint, rope or chalk to mark the lines

The aim of the game is to dismiss as many of the opposing team as possible, within a given time. The time limit may vary depending on the numbers taking part: usually each game takes approximately ten to fifteen minutes, but it can be repeated several times in the same afternoon without palling.

Divide the players into two teams. About fifteen on each team is ideal, but in a slightly longer area, with more balls in play, greater numbers are possible. Mark out the course and position the players as shown in the diagram. Two players from each team stand inside tramlines behind the opposition. Players cannot go outside their allotted areas. If anyone crosses a line unlawfully to get the ball, a free pass is given to the opposing side.

Two balls are thrown into the main area. The teams attempt to throw the balls over the heads of the opposition to their fellow team members behind them. Meanwhile, the other side tries to intercept the balls and prevent them from reaching the tramlines. The players in the tramlines try to hit their opponents below the knee. If someone is hit below the knee, he joins his fellow team members in the tramlines and continues to try to get the other team out. The game continues until everyone is out, on one side or the other.

14 Falling dominoes

No equipment needed

This game is ideal for large groups.

The players form several equally numbered teams and line up, one behind the other, all facing the same way. At the starting signal, the first player in each team squats. Immediately the second player squats, and the third, and so on right down to the last person in the team. No one can squat until the person in front of them is in full squat position. Then, when the last person in the line squats, he immediately stands up again, and the process happens in reverse order as the whole team stands up, one by one. No one can stand until the person behind is standing up. The winning team is the first to complete the sequence. Play the game several times.

To vary the game and heighten the excitement, assign a colour to a team (eg black, red) and, as each player goes down, he shouts out his team colour and the number he is in the line. So, as the players squat, they call out, 'Black one down', 'Black two down', 'Black three down', and so on. On the return journey, they shout, 'Black twenty up', 'Black nineteen up'...

15 Fire! Fire!

You will need:

Two identical buckets for each team, one filled with water
A supply of plastic cups

Any number of teams can compete. Each team lines up in single file, with a bucket of water at one end of the line and an empty bucket at the other. Each team member has a cup. The object is to pass the water by transferring it from one cup to another down the line. The team to get the most water into the empty bucket is the winner.

- 12 -

16 Handball

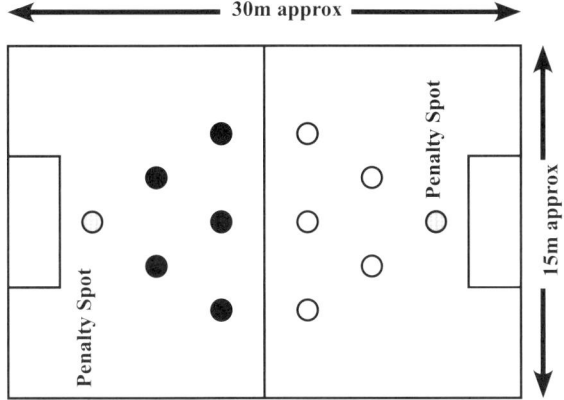

You will need:

A large ball, football size, preferably plastic, inflated well for maximum bounce
Masking tape, paint, rope or chalk to mark out the playing area

The playing area should be rectangular in shape, and should be approx 30 m x 15 m, although this can be adapted for indoor play. The only markings required are the centre line, the penalty spot and the goal boxes. Have six or more players in each team. The tallest team member acts as the main central defender, and another acts as goalkeeper. The rest of the team may attack or defend as required.

The teams line up as shown in the diagram, with each team attacking towards their own goalkeeper. The referee throws the ball into the centre, and the team who wins possession advances towards their goalkeeper, dribbling the ball (as in basketball, three paces being allowed before the ball must be passed to another player), throwing, rolling or bouncing it to a team mate. Meanwhile, the defence tries to stop them from scoring by picking up loose passes and goal attempts. The defence may also try to block the view of the goalkeeper (this is allowed as long as defenders don't step inside the goal box, see 'Fouls').

When a player reaches her team's goal box, she throws the ball to the goalkeeper, over the heads of the defence or through a space where a defender has been caught out of position. A goal is scored if the goalkeeper catches the ball within the box and without it touching the ground. If, however, the ball bounces or the goalkeeper drops the ball, no goal is scored (see 'Out of play').

Fouls

A free throw, from the point of infringement, should be awarded to the other team:
- when players kick the ball
- when players make bodily contact with members of the opposition, ie tripping, pushing, pulling, kicking.

A penalty throw, from the penalty spot, is awarded to a team if a defender from the opposition steps inside their goal box. The thrower stands on the penalty spot, the goalkeeper is inside his goal box, and a nominated defender is allowed to stand in front of the goalkeeper (as long as he is not inside the box). The defender attempts to stop or divert the ball, or to obstruct the view of the goalkeeper so that he fails to catch the ball and drops it.

If an attacker steps inside the goal box, the defending side may take a throw-in from the goal line (see 'Out of play'). A throw is also awarded when the goalkeeper drops the ball in a goal attempt. If the goal-line is a wall, the player should stand against it to throw. If the goal line has a space behind it, the player should stand behind it.

Out of play

The touch-line is the line running down the side of the pitch. When the ball goes over the touch-line and out of play, the offending team forfeits possession and the other team throws the ball back into play.

The goal-line is the line behind the goal-box. When the ball goes over the goal-line, the defending team throws the ball into play, irrespective of who touched the ball last.

- 13 -

17 Indian-file dodge ball

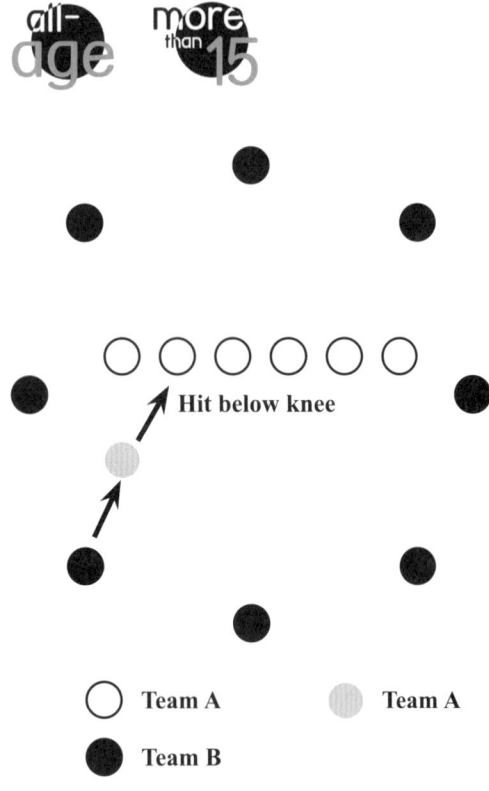

You will need:

One fairly soft, light ball

The players arrange themselves as shown. Inside the circle of players, five or six others arrange themselves in file, grasping each other by the waist or the shoulders. The whole file is free to move in any direction, but their grip on each other must not be broken. The players in the circle try to hit the last person in the file below the knee with a ball. The ball should be passed around or across the circle to someone who is best placed to have a shot, and should not just be thrown haphazardly by anyone. The player who scores a hit goes to the front of the file and the person who was hit takes his place in the circle.

18 Informal skittle ball

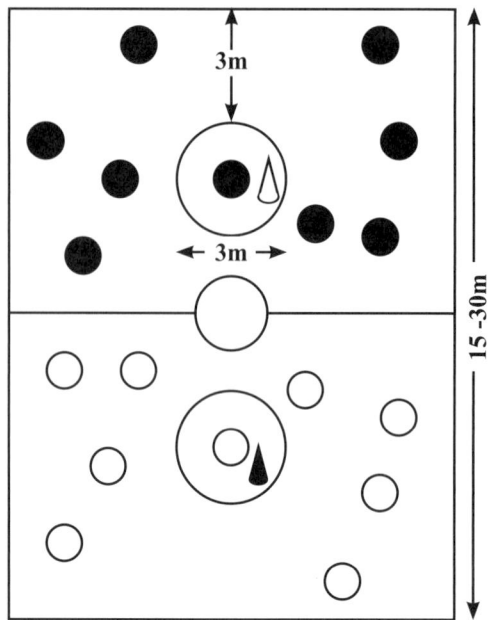

You will need:

A ball
Skittles about 70 cm high (the same number for each team)

This is a simple quick-moving game with few rules, suitable for indoor or outdoor play. Mark the court as shown in the diagram. Form two teams of equal numbers. The object of the game is to knock over the opposing team's skittles with the ball. When a skittle is upset, the attacking team scores two points. If a defending goalkeeper knocks over his own skittles, the opposition scores one point. The rules are simple:

1. The ball must be only passed by hand. It may not be carried for more than two paces or held for more than two seconds. It may be dribbled, however, by pat-bouncing or volleying with the hands.
2. No tackling or rough play of any kind is allowed.
3. The goalkeeper must remain inside her circle, and attackers must on no account step inside the circle.

A penalty throw is awarded for any infringement of rules 2 and 3. The throw is taken from the centre of the playing area, and directed at an unguarded skittle. If the skittle is knocked over, three points are awarded to the attacking team.

19 Information collecting

You will need:

Paper, pencils and information lists

Groups of children must be supervised by adults.

Each group is given a 'shopping list' of information (preferably useful) to collect within a given (perhaps local) area. You may also want to set a time limit. The winning group is the first to return with all the information requested.

20 Pick-up sticks

You will need:

Thirty or so garden canes, or similar, painted red, blue, yellow, green, black and white

Assign different scores to each colour. This is a good game for small groups.

A player bundles all the sticks together and lets them drop gently onto the floor in a random pile. Each player in turn tries to pick up a stick at a time without moving any of the others. If another stick moves, the player loses his turn and the stick he has picked up is not counted to his score.

21 Jump kangaroo

You will need:

A strong piece of string 3–4m long
A very soft ball, eg a ball of wool

This is a very old game, simple but always a great favourite.

Tie the ball securely to the string. A player stands in the centre of a circle of players and swings the ball fairly low to the ground, about 0.25 m above ground-level. The players in the circle then move in about 0.5 m. While the swinger continues to swing, they are forced to jump to avoid being hit. Anyone the ball touches is out. The game speeds up as the ball is swung faster and faster!

After a few minutes, change the direction and the swinger to avoid dizziness. For more athletic groups, the swinging ball may be raised or lowered, or swung at different speeds.

22 Nature trail

You will need:

A ruler for each team

This game is best played in a garden with trees. Form two or more teams with equal numbers in each. Appoint a referee to ensure fair play and accurate measurements! Each team elects a captain who always stays at home base. The teams then go in search of objects which they have to bring back to their captain. He asks them for three objects each time, eg a 50 mm blade of grass, an elm leaf, a feather. The team is given one minute or less to find the items. When they have finished the task, the captain calls out the next three items to be collected. Points are allotted for each correct item.

The game may be further complicated by adding 'burdens' to the collectors, eg during the search the team must carry one of their number piggyback fashion, or they should all hop on one foot.

23 Nehemiah's wall

You will need:

Boxes, sellotaped so as to be fairly rigid

Divide the players into two teams. Two people from each team act as the wall builders, the others supply them with boxes with which to build. The two teams line up behind the starting line, each with a pile of boxes. The two wall builders position themselves approximately 20 m away from the starting line, in front of their respective teams.

The first player in each team carries two boxes to the wall builders, then returns to the starting line. The second player takes another two boxes and returns, and so on, until all boxes have been delivered. The wall builders construct a wall as they receive the boxes. The winning team is the one with the highest wall.

24 Sea battle

You will need:

Four small balls of different coloured wool
Small white cards, with the letters D, S or B clearly written on each
A white card for each fleet, with the letter B and a flag drawn on it

Divide the players into four fleets. Each fleet has an admiral, a quartermaster and a base in which they both sit. Assign a colour to each fleet, and loosely tie a piece of wool of that colour around the wrists of its members. Give pieces of wool in their fleet's colour to each of the quartermasters.

There are three types of ships in a fleet: battleships, submarines and destroyers. Give the players a card each to indicate which ship they represent. For every three destroyers, there should be two submarines and one battleship. During battle, a battleship beats a destroyer; a destroyer beats a submarine; and a submarine beats a battleship. These facts should be made very clear to the children.

At a given signal, the fleets are released from their bases to a central fighting area, where each ship challenges another from a different fleet by touching her. The two then show their cards to indicate the kinds of ship they are. When they are the same, nothing happens and they both sail off to challenge other ships. However, when they are different, the loser must give up her piece of wool to the other and return to base for a new piece of wool from the quartermaster. The winning fleet is the one to collect the most wool from the others.

This game can be played for up to thirty minutes by virtually any number of players. It is advisable to have half-time in order to change the players into different ships and give them different cards.

To vary the game, give one of the battleships in each fleet the extra card with the flag on it to indicate that it is the flagship. The flagship is worth 50–150 pieces of wool, depending on the number of players there are in a fleet. If the flagship is attacked by a submarine, it must surrender the flag too, which the submarine at once returns to his admiral. The admiral passes it to his own flagship, which thus becomes doubly valuable, worth 100–300 pieces of wool. If this flagship is attacked, it loses both its flags simultaneously. Clearly it becomes wise for the flagships to play a defensive role and to be protected by the submarines and destroyers in its fleet. The flagship can only be changed at half-time.

The arduous job of counting the wool should be left to the end, when all the ships hand in their captured wool to their quartermasters.

25 Simon says

No equipment needed

This is an old and simple game that produces a great deal of enjoyment. Someone is chosen to be 'Simon' (or he may use his own name). Any command Simon gives must be obeyed only if it is prefaced with the words 'Simon says...'

The players line up and Simon commences, eg 'Simon says, quick march!' – all the players march around; 'Simon says, hands up!' – the players raise their hands. However, if this is followed by 'Hands down', their hands must stay up because the order wasn't prefaced with 'Simon says...' Anyone who makes the mistake of putting their hands down is out.

26 Piggyback jousting

You will need:

Half a dozen thin plastic bags filled with water
Half a dozen poles
A wooden broomstick (or similar) for each team

Space the poles at intervals along a measured

course. Secure each pole in an upright position, and tie the water-filled bags to the top.

The teams line up in pairs at starting line, one of the pair riding his partner piggyback fashion. Each piggyback pair is given a jousting pole (the broomstick). On the signal 'Go', the pair set off down the course and, as they go, the rider tries to burst the bags in sequence. A pair cannot proceed past a pole without first breaking the bag. The first pair to complete the course is the winner.

27 Plank race

You will need:

A stout plank of wood
Masking tape, paint, rope or chalk to mark out the race course

This race is best run as a relay. Mark out a course approximately 30 m long. The players form teams of three, or multiples of three if it is a relay.

On the command 'Go', two members of a team carry the third, seated on the plank, to the end of course. As soon as they get there, the next three take up the challenge and run back to the starting line. The race continues until all the threes have run. The first team to finish is the winner.

28 Press-gang chain

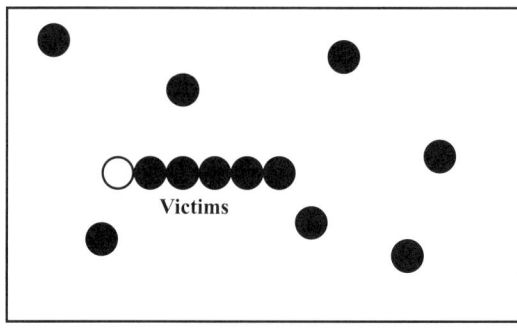

No equipment needed

Players scatter around a large lawn or field. A press-gang leader is chosen, who whizzes around the playing area catching victims. Once touched, they join the press-gang by linking arms. Escaping players are gradually caught and join on. The last person to remain untagged is the winner.

29 Random handball

You will need:

A frido football

Divide players into two equal teams. The game begins with a member of one team tossing a ball to one of his own side. The aim is for one team to keep possession of the ball for as long as possible, while the other tries to intercept and gain possession of it. Every time the ball is caught, the members of that team (except the player who catches the ball) clap their hands and stamp their feet.

30 Rounders

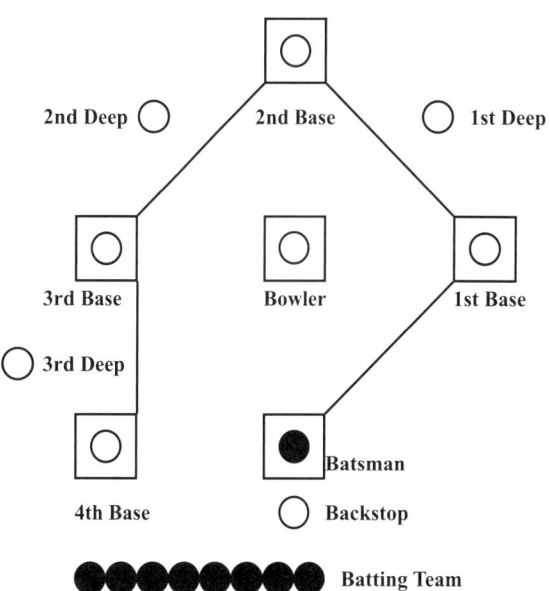

You will need:

Rounders sticks, a rounders ball or tennis ball
Four bases or posts

Form two teams of nine players. One team bats while the opponents field. Fielders are given the following positions: bowler; backstop; 1st, 2nd, 3rd and 4th bases; 1st, 2nd and 3rd deeps.

The bowler bowls underarm to the batsman; the ball must be between the batsman's shoulder and his knee. The batsman runs to first base whether or not he hits the ball. He is out if the ball is caught or the base to which he is running is 'trumped' before he reaches it. Fielders must have the ball in their possession and must make direct contact with the base in order to get a batsman out.

At no time should there be more than one batsman at a base. If this occurs, the first batsman to have arrived at the base is out. Batsmen must stop running from base to base as soon as the bowler has the ball and is standing in the bowler's square.

If the batsman hits the ball and runs round the pitch, he gains a rounder. If he gets around without having first hit the ball, he scores half a rounder. A team continues to bat until everyone is out. Two innings are usually played in rounders.

31 Scavenger hunt

For reasons of child safety, adult supervisors should be able to see each child in the defined area of play.

Form pairs or groups, and give each a list of objects which they must collect within a specified time. The first back with all the objects are the winners. The objects will depend on local surroundings, eg particular flowers, leaves, grasses, insects, shells, pebbles.

32 Shunting tunnel

You will need:

A large soft toy, ball or cushion

Divide 40+ players into equally numbered teams. Each team forms two lines so that everyone is facing a partner. Hands are criss-crossed, and it is important to keep close to your neighbours.

The object to be shunted is placed across the arms of the first pair at one end, and is gently bounced and shunted down the 'tunnel'. When it reaches the end, the last pair grab it, run round to the front and begin shunting the object down the tunnel again. When the original first pair are back at the front, and the shunted object has completed its final trip down, the whole team sits, the first to do so being the winner.

33 Soccer slalom

You will need:

Several pairs of large wellington boots
One football for each team
Wooden or plastic poles
Water

Make a slalom course by spacing the poles about a metre apart in a straight line. Wearing outsized wellies filled with water, team members have to weave in and out of the poles, dribbling a football. Having completed the course, each player picks up the ball, runs back and passes it to the next player, who repeats the process. The last member of the team to complete the course collects the poles on his return journey and brings them back to the base line. A steward should be allocated to each line, to ensure that players slalom the course correctly.

34 Spaceship

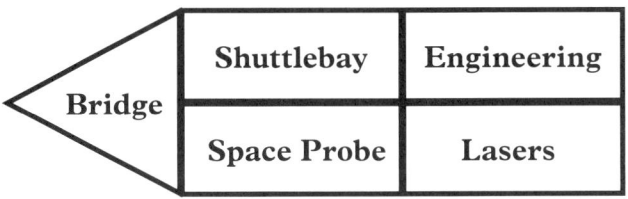

You will need:

> *Masking tape, paint, rope or chalk to mark out the spaceship*

Probably thirty to fifty is the maximum number of players for this game, but this will depend on the size of the playing area.

Mark out the space as shown in the diagram and label the different areas, to make the ship. The bridge is out of bounds and anyone who touches it is out, as is anyone who touches the space outside the ship. The leader calls out a section of the ship, and the players have to get there as fast as possible; the last one (or two or three) is out.

To vary the game, other special commands may include: 'Red alert!', when the players sit down with their heads between their knees; 'Go into warp drive', when they lie down with their heads pointing towards the bridge; and 'Prepare for landing', when they lie down with their heads towards the launchpad.

35 Stand up!

No equipment needed

Divide players into two or more equally numbered teams. The teams form pairs and stand back to back, with their arms linked. On the command 'Stand up', the pairs have to stand without unlinking their arms. The first pair to stand is awarded points. Set a time limit for completing the standing-up process.

Next, two pairs from the same team combine to make a four. Fours sit back to back, with linked arms, and repeat the standing-up process. The first four to stand are awarded more points. Another pair from the same team join the four, and so on... Keep adding pairs. Each time a new pair is added to the group, the game gets harder. Any group that does not manage to stand within the time limit is out. The winning group is the one which, at the end, has the most points.

36 Three-legged fun

You will need:

> *Old tights or stockings (or similar) with which to tie people's legs*

Three-legged activities could include a three-legged race, football, handball, rounders or netball.

37 Twin tug of war

You will need:

> *Two strong ropes*
> *Masking tape, paint, rope or chalk to mark the circle*

Tie the ropes in the middle so as to have four ends of equal length. Divide players into four teams. Mark out a circle on the ground and position each team outside the circle, giving them one end of a rope each.

On the starter's signal, all the teams begin to pull. When one team is pulled across the circle line, it is eliminated from the game. Restart the game; when another team is eliminated, the remaining two compete against each other, using the circle as the penalty area.

38 Volleyball (a simple version)

Fig 1

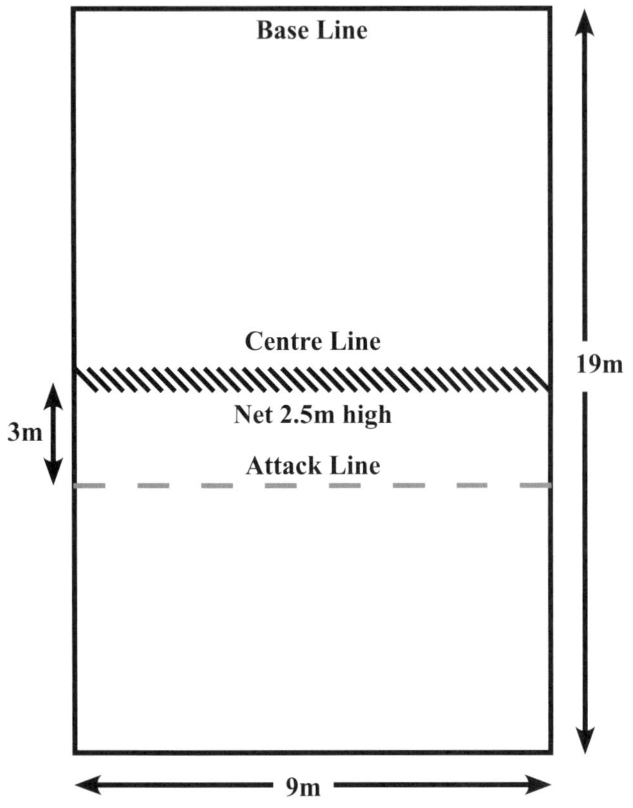

[Court diagram: Base Line, Centre Line, Net 2.5m high, Attack Line; 19m × 9m; 3m from centre line to attack line]

You will need:

A good quality light ball, eg a frido ball or football

This is an energetic game demanding teamwork and the appreciation of others. The fun increases with the level of skill. The playing area is rectangular, approximately 19x9 m (Fig 1, though a smaller area could be used); a tennis court would be suitable. The playing area is divided into two equal sized courts by a centre line. The net across the centre is 1 m deep, and the top should be about 2.5 m from the ground. However, the net could be lowered for beginners and children.

Fig 2

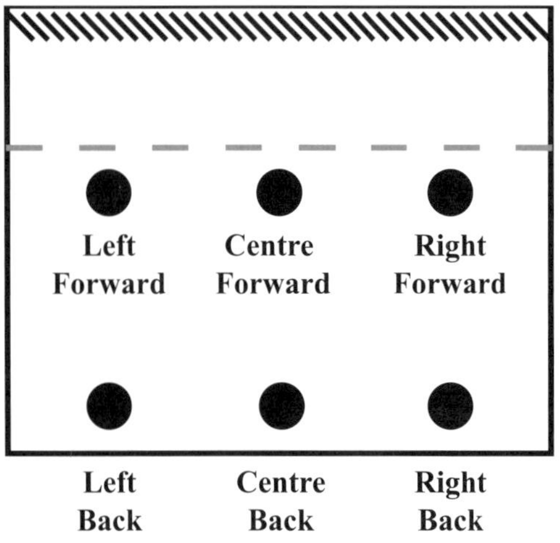

[Diagram showing six player positions: Left Forward, Centre Forward, Right Forward, Left Back, Centre Back, Right Back]

Officially, volleyball is played by a six-person team (Fig 2), but the game can be adapted for a larger number. Divide the players into two teams. The aim for each team is to make the ball hit the ground or be mishandled on their opponents' side of the net, while keeping it aloft on their own side.

The player in the right back position starts the game by serving from behind the back line of the court (Fig 3). He serves by tossing the ball into the air and hitting it with any part of his hand, fist or arm (Fig 4). He must not step over the back line into the playing area until the ball has been served. The ball must go over the net without anyone else in his team hitting it. Meanwhile, the other team try to block the ball and send it back.

Fig 3

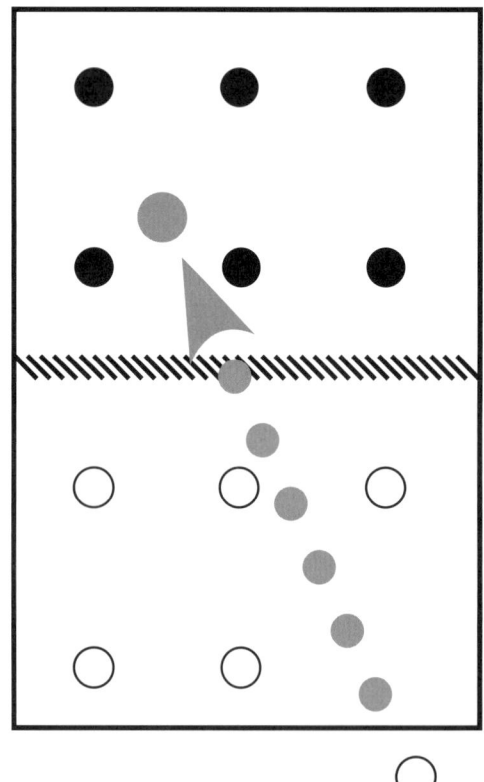

Once the ball is in play, any player can pass the ball to someone on his own side, or he can send it back immediately in the hope of scoring a goal by the ball hitting the playing area. A player should not hold on to the ball once play is in motion, nor should he touch the ball twice in succession. Players are not allowed to touch the net or to extend their hands over it, and it is deemed an offence if the ball passes under the net. Players may overstep the side and back boundaries of the court to return a ball, and their feet may touch the centre line but must not cross it. The opponents' side must not be 'invaded'.

Fig 4

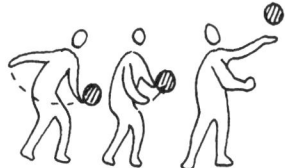

Whenever a team takes over the service, each player rotates on position in a clockwise direction. A team loses service, and their opponents gain a point, when the ball touches the playing area. If the ball goes out of bounds, hits any obstruction or fails to clear the net, the serve is lost and no points are scored for either side. If any offence is committed, the ball should be given to the other side to recommence the game.

There are books available for those keen to play volley ball at a higher level, and there is also an Amateur Volleyball Association.

39 Water wide game

over-8s | more than 15 | lots of space | messy | team game

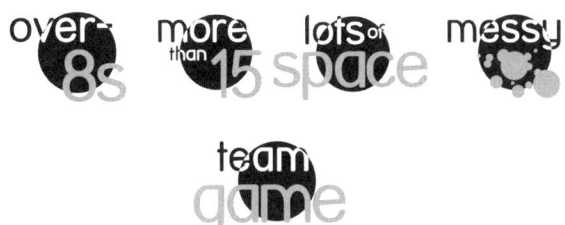

You will need:

About 100 marbles or peas
Squeezy bottles for most players
Plenty of water
Two colours of breakable wool
Masking tape, paint, rope or chalk to mark the bases

This game can be played by up to sixty people. You will need to set a time limit.

Players form two teams. Each team is assigned a colour and a base approximately 3.5 m in radius. The bases are about 175 m apart and in full view of each other. Wool in the team colour is loosely tied to the wrists of team members; the wool constitutes a life. Equal amounts of marbles and more wool are placed inside each base. The aim is for the players to invade the other team's base to steal their marbles, and to defend their own base by attempting to tag the invaders. If a player is tagged by a member of the other team before entering a base, she loses her life and has to give up her wool and return to base to get a new one. Players are not allowed to enter their own bases except to get a new life. If a player reaches her opponents' base with wool intact, she can take a marble. But if her wool 'life' is taken on the way back, she must surrender the marble also. The team with the most marbles at the end is the winner.

To add to the fun, as well as tagging, teams can defend their bases by squirting water in their opponents' faces in the hope of slowing them down. In the ensuing melee, leaders may find themselves under attack and utterly soaked! Make sure plenty of water is available. If there aren't enough squeezy bottles to go round, you could allow teams to plunder each other for bottles.

40 Wheelbarrow marathon

over-8s | messy | team game

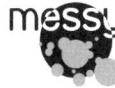

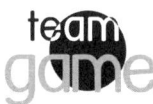

You will need:

Small plastic bowls of jelly or custard
Masking tape, paint, rope or chalk to mark the tracks

Divide players into two teams. Mark out a racetrack for each team, and place the bowls of jelly or custard at intervals along it. The track is covered in relays. Each team forms into pairs, and the pairs form wheelbarrows – one person holds another by the legs while he crawls along on his hands. As the pair reach a bowl, the 'wheelbarrow' has to eat the jelly or custard in it; he is not allowed to move on until he has done so. The next pair in a team can only set off when the pair before them have completed the course. Replace the bowls as and when their contents are eaten. When all the pairs in a team have finished, that team is declared the winner.

2 Parachute games

Introduction to Parachute Canopy Games and Play

A circular canopy or parachute 4–8 m in diameter is a resourceful piece of equipment for involving a large group of children in co-operative play activities. It encourages team work and togetherness. Parachute games are best played with children aged 5 and upwards.

The games will work best if attention is given to spacing the players evenly around the canopy. Players grip the edge of the canopy with clenched fists, knuckles on top, around the perimeter. It is a good idea to practise raising the canopy and allowing it to fall several times, before starting to play any games:

- Everyone holds the canopy taut and still, at waist level.
- Moving together, they raise the canopy and allow it to fall once or twice. This is best done to a steady count, ie 'one, two, three, lift', so that everyone lifts at the same time. Don't pull the canopy down each time, but allow it to fall naturally so that it billows upward. On the third lift, get the players to stretch as high as they can, so that the canopy billows up above them. Then get each player to take one or more steps in towards the middle, still holding the canopy, creating a mushroom shape. As the canopy collapses, move back out. Practise this basic co-ordination until everyone is co-operating and beginning to develop a team spirit.

Safety

Check the ground underneath where you are planning to hold the parachute games. Grass is by far the best surface, but it needs to be dry, not slippery. If you are playing the games indoors, use a non-splinter floor if children are going to remove their shoes. Give clear warnings about looking out for other people when going under the canopy, so that there aren't too many bumped heads! A leader needs to be in charge even when young people are contributing games ideas, and it is essential that all players listen and obey instructions so that no injuries occur. The presence of a second adult is helpful, to field balls and generally assist in encouraging the players and maintaining control.

Caution

Do not use the canopy for tossing children. It is particularly dangerous to play games which involve using the canopy like a trampoline, with the margin held taut and the 'victim' bounced in the middle. The player cannot see or feel where the ground is, and it is all too easy for him to hit hard ground if the canopy is slackened, with consequent injury to spine or head. Even games involving walking on a tight parachute are to be avoided, as it is possible to damage an ankle by sudden unexpected contact with the ground even when the drop is only 10 cm or less.

The material used for parachutes and play canopies is often highly inflammable. Use it with care and keep away from fires, barbecues, cigarettes etc.

Balls are often used to play canopy activities. Sponge balls or light, vinyl footballs are best.

41 Battle ball

You will need:

A sponge ball or vinyl football

If your canopy has different coloured segments, divide it into two equal halves according to colour. Players should hold the canopy at approximately waist height.

The leader throws the ball into the centre of the canopy. Two teams of players, each holding one half of the canopy, compete to try to bounce the ball so that it comes off the canopy on their opponents' side. The canopy should be kept tight at all times, with players keeping both hands on the perimeter, working as a team to move it. Kicking the ball from underneath is not allowed, neither may the ball be handled. (Handling counts as a point to the other side.)

42 Canopy volleyball

You will need:

Two canopies
A ball
A net

If two canopies are available, divide the players into two teams, each holding one canopy, and position them on either side of a net. The aim of the game is to toss the ball from one canopy, over the net, to touch the ground on the opponents' side. Teams must try not to let the ball touch the ground on their side (as in volleyball), using their canopy to catch the ball and throw it back over the net.

43 Cat and mouse

You will need:

Some wrapped sweets

Hold the canopy at shoulder height, making sure there is a space between each player around the perimeter. A sweet is placed under the centre of the canopy, on the floor, and the canopy is lowered. Choose one player to be the cat and another to be the mouse. They stand outside the perimeter circle.

On the count of three, the players lift the canopy. They continue to count loudly up to twenty, as the mouse runs around the canopy trying to avoid the cat, before making a dash under the canopy to grab the sweet. The cat cannot enter the space under the canopy until the mouse does. If the pursuing cat catches the mouse before he can escape with the 'goodies', the mouse is out and joins the group holding the canopy.

If the cat fails to catch the mouse, he is replaced by another player. When the children reach twenty, the canopy comes down. If it comes down on top of the cat or mouse, then one or both are replaced by other players. Score one point to the cat if the mouse is caught, and one point to the mouse if the sweet is taken.

44 Heads and tails

You will need:

A large circular 'coin' 30–35 cm in diameter, made out of card, with a head on one side and tail on the other

In a circle, the players hold the canopy taut at waist level, with the 'coin' in the centre. Number them one and two alternately round the circle. All those numbered one try, by working together in bouncing the canopy, to make sure that the coin is tails up; all those numbered two try to keep it heads up.

45 Making a tent

The players lift the parachute and let it fall once or twice. On the third lift, they all take one step forward, while the parachute is billowing, and then bring the fabric down taut behind them. They then sit on the edge of the chute, thus creating a sort of tent with everybody underneath. This is a useful technique for getting everybody's attention when storytelling, giving instructions, etc.

46 Mushroom

All the players stand around the edge of the canopy, holding it at waist level. The leader shouts, 'Mushroom!', and everyone lifts the canopy until it mushrooms up in the air. The leader shouts out a category, eg all girls, all boys, those wearing red, those with blue eyes, everyone who had cornflakes for breakfast. Those who fit that category let go of the canopy and run underneath it to the opposite side. Those not running keep hold of the canopy and bring it down as usual. Slow runners may get caught under the canopy when it comes down, but this only adds to the fun.

47 Punch ball

You will need:

Several large, lightweight balls

Hold the canopy at waist height. Place three or four balls on top of it, and choose two or three players to go underneath. Their task is to try to knock the balls off the canopy, while the people holding it keep the balls bouncing in the middle. From time to time, replace the players underneath the canopy.

48 Roller coaster

You will need:

A large lightweight ball

This co-operative activity demands quite a bit of concentration, but the game is good fun and very satisfying.

By gently lifting and dropping the edges of the canopy, a 'Mexican wave' effect is created. Place the ball on the canopy and try to roll it around the perimeter edge smoothly. On a given signal, change the direction of the ball. See how many complete circles the team can achieve. This can be played as a team competition.

49 Shoe scramble

You will need:

Players to be wearing shoes

Number each player around the circle from one to six. All the 'number one' players remove a shoe and throw it under the canopy. On the count of three, the canopy is lifted and lowered twice, then mushroomed up on the third lift. Those missing a shoe must go into the middle, retrieve it and get back to their places before the canopy descends. Those who fail go in a second time with the next round of players. The same continues until every number has had a turn and all the shoes are retrieved.

50 Storytelling

Storytelling or saying nursery rhymes with the aid of a parachute can help a group to learn participation and co-operation. You have their attention because they are standing still holding the chute and there is scope for creativity as players think of actions that give visual aids to the story.

The story of Goldilocks and the three bears could be started as follows: 'There were once three bears, great big Daddy Bear (make a high mushroom effect) Mummy Bear (make a smaller mushroom) and Baby Bear (just a little billowing)' etc.

Bible stories and parables can also be told with a parachute as an aid:

'One day Jesus and his friends went out in a boat on the Sea of Galilee. Little waves lapped at the shore (set up minute ripples with the taut chute held down low). They all climbed into the boat and it set out into deeper water. The sea was very still, with not a wave in sight (chute held taut and motionless). The disciples, who were used to boats, soon settled down. Then a gentle wind began to blow, ruffling the smooth water (chute gently moves). Slowly the waves got bigger and bigger, and theirs was just a little tiny boat tossing around on a rough sea (suit actions to story). By now, the boat was pitching up and down, and the disciples were terrified. A great storm had blown up (lift the chute into a mushroom). The disciples woke Jesus up in a panic. He stood up, looked at the boisterous waves (chute moving in wave actions), and told them to be still. He commanded the wind to stop – and suddenly all was calm (chute held taut quickly). The disciples were amazed. They had been frightened of the storm, but now they felt frightened of Jesus as they realised just how powerful their friend was.'

51 Swap

Number the players round the circle from one to six. On the count of three, raise and lower the canopy twice as usual, and, on the third lift, shout out a number (between one and six). The children with that number have to swap places under the billowing canopy before it falls. Tell them beforehand to head for gaps around the edge, to keep their eyes open and to avoid bumping into one another. Make sure that those who remain around the edge allow the canopy to fall slowly rather than pulling it down hard.

52 Turtle

Imagine the canopy is the shell of a turtle. Everybody gets underneath, holding the canopy above them, facing outwards. They then all move in one direction, making sure that the shell never loses its shape. Try putting obstacles in the way for the group to get round or climb over, again making sure that the shell never changes shape.

3 Sports day ideas

The element of competition and excitement can sometimes be exaggerated on sports day, so it is essential that children are adequately supervised and safety rules are carefully followed. The ideas in this section are suitable for players aged 8+.

53 Camel race

No equipment needed

This is a race over a given length of track appropriate to the age group. It is played in groups of three: one person is the camel's head; another makes its back and holds the waist of the 'head'; the third is the rider who sits on the 'back' with his arms extended so that they are placed on the shoulders of the 'head'.

The object is to race to the finishing line without the rider falling off or the camel parts being separated. In the event of riders taking a tumble, they can remount provided that the camel is stationary.

54 Cross-country motorama

You will need:

    Some old car tyres for each team,
    Some marker sticks
    Optional obstacles made with planks and boxes
    A hand flag
    Marking tape, paint or chalk to mark the course

Divide the players into teams. Lay out the course and give clear instructions as to the obstacles. Mark out some pit stops: these are places where one player passes on the tyre to the next. A little imagination in layout and obstacles can give this game great spectator value.

The race begins at a starting line. When the flag is dropped, a player in each team rolls a tyre down the course to the first pit stop, where the next player takes over, driving the tyre to the next pit stop, where another player takes over, and so on to the end of the marked course. The first tyre and team to pass the finishing post is the winner.

If obstacles are added to the course, there will need to be careful supervision at each obstacle to ensure that the order in which drivers arrive is the order in which they go over or under the obstacle.

55 Goliath ball

You will need:

A large ball 2–3 m in diameter (these are available commercially)
Masking tape, paint or chalk to mark out a pitch

This is a fun game for all ages and any number of players. There are several versions and it can be adapted to suit local circumstances. The field of play can vary in size and should be marked according to the plan shown although all dimensions indicated in the diagram may be adapted depending on the playing area available.

Two linesmen should be appointed, one on each side of the field of play, who can also stop the game by signalling to the referee when they wish to draw his attention to any incident that occurs during the game. The game is played by two teams of equal numbers – ideally, ten to fifteen players in each. The teams form a kind of rugby scrum to push the ball goalwards. Meanwhile, a captain controls each team from a back position. Agree on a time limit: ten to fifteen minutes each way is a maximum. Change ends at half-time and include an interval of about four minutes.

The winners of the toss may choose which way they wish to play. The ball is placed in the centre of the field of play, with the players standing on their respective defence lines. The game commences with the players running for the ball from their starting positions. A goal is scored when the ball has passed between the goal-posts or marks indicated on the goal-lines. The team scoring the greater number of goals is the winner. If no goals are scored, or if the goal scores are equal, the game can be decided on points. If one side succeeds in pushing the ball over the goal-line between the goalposts, they score three points. If they push the ball over the goal-line but not between the posts, they score two points. In either case, the ball is then replaced in the centre of the field of play, and the game continues.

If the ball crosses either of the touch-lines, the game is restarted with the ball placed on the 9m lines opposite the point of crossing and all the players standing 4m from it. If, during a scrum, the ball remains stationary for longer than one minute, the game is restarted, with all the players standing 4 m from the ball.

Any player holding on to the lace of the ball, kicking or punching an opponent, jumping on or kicking the ball or an opponent, penalises his side. The game is stopped by the referee and the offending team made to stand 9m away from the ball, facing their own goal, while the opposing team pushes off when the whistle is blown. In the event of any of the defending team being penalised in the goal area, one player only from the penalised team is allowed to stand in the goal; the rest must stand on the goal-line at either side of the posts. The ball is placed on the goal area line, opposite the centre of the goal, with all players of the attacking team behind the ball.

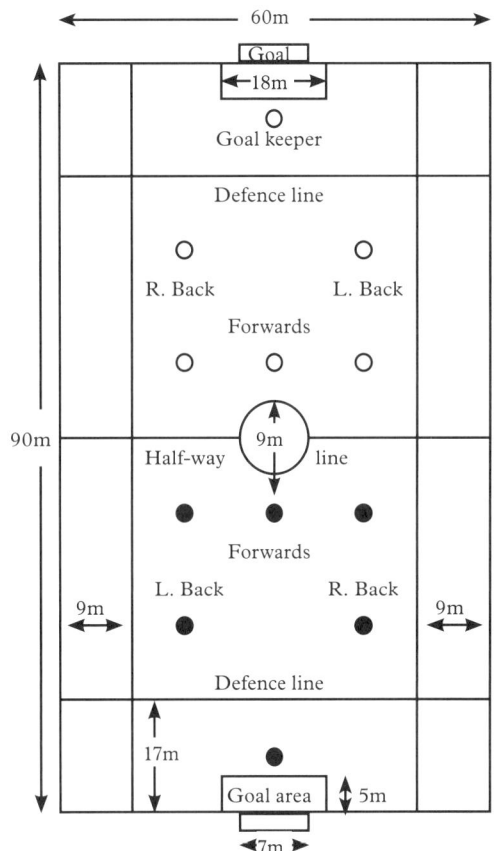

56 Obstacle race

lots of space

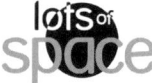

You will need:

A variety of obstacles, eg tarpaulins, pipes, car tyres, benches, planks

Any variety of obstacles can be arranged over a given racecourse, but make sure that they are compatible with the ability of your group. Suggestions are:

- Crawling under a tarpaulin which is pegged to the ground
- Crawling through large pipes
- Passing through suspended car tyres
- Walking along a plank or balance bench
- Climbing over two bales of straw or a bench

57 Rugby scrum

over-8s team game

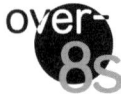

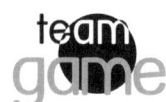

You will need:

Masking tape to mark a box and a dividing line

Two even teams 'set down' into a scrum, rugby fashion, inside the box, over the dividing line. The team pushing their opponents back over the edge of the box are the winners. This game must be played at least twice so that the teams can change ends.

58 Tunnel relay

lots of space team game

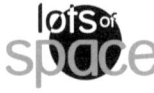

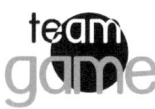

You will need:

A tunnel made of canvas or stout cloth about 600cm long and 90cm in diameter

Two teams enter the tunnel at opposite ends. Only two players are allowed in the tunnel at any time. The inevitable passing point can give plenty of spectator value. The first team with every member clear of the tunnel is the winner.

59 Welly throwing

lots of space

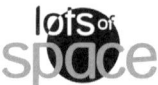

You will need:

A wellington boot

This game is very like discus throwing except, of course, the wellington boot substitutes for a discus. The player with the longest throw is the winner. Handicaps, such as throwing with the left hand, may be introduced for variation.

60 Wheelbarrow race

over-8s

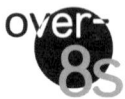

No equipment needed.

Divide players into pairs. One player walks on her hands while her partner holds her legs up behind as if wheeling a wheelbarrow. The course should be fairly short.

4 Indoor games for the very young

Many young children attend nursery schools and 'mums and toddlers' groups. They enjoy physical activities such as hopping, jumping and clapping games. Young children are not usually competitive but appreciate using their imagination, pretending and singing. Through simple games, they can begin to experience the need and the joy of working together, and appreciating others. Action stories, in which the youngest can take some part, are popular with this age group. They will usually happily follow their leaders.

61 Ball catching

You will need:

  A large, soft ball

About eight to ten children stand in a circle. The leader stands in the middle with a large ball which she throws to each child in turn. When a child drops the ball, he or she has a turn in the middle.

62 Bouncing ball

No equipment needed

Invite the children to join in with the words and actions of this rhyme:
  I'm like a great big bouncing ball *(jumping)*,
  High in the air, then down I fall *(fall down)*.
  Now I run along the ground *(running)*,
  Now I'm turning round and round and round *(spinning action)*.

63 Catching tails

You will need:

  Pieces of ribbon or tape, one for each pair.

Divide the children into pairs. One of the pair has a 'tail' (a piece of ribbon) tucked into their clothes at the back. At a signal the children with 'tails' rush off. Their partners follow them and try to catch 'tail'. When a 'tail' is caught, pairs skip around together, holding the ribbon.

- 29 -

64 Quiet please

No equipment needed

This is a good game to restore quietness after a noisy game. The children lie in a comfortable position on the floor. The aim is for them to lie completely still for a given period of time. Anyone caught moving is out; the last one left in is the winner.

65 The farmer's in his den

No equipment needed

The children form a circle, with one in the middle who is the farmer. They sing:

The farmer's in his den,
The farmer's in his den,
E I E I O
The farmer's in his den.

The farmer wants a wife,
The farmer wants a wife, etc.
The 'farmer' picks a 'wife' from the children in the circle (their sex is immaterial!).

The wife wants a child, etc.
The 'wife' picks a 'child' from the children in the circle.

The child wants a nurse, etc.
The 'child' picks a 'nurse' from the children in the circle.

The nurse wants a dog, etc.
The 'nurse' picks a 'dog' from the children in the circle.

The dog wants a bone, etc.
The 'dog' picks a 'bone' from the children in the circle.

We all pat the dog, etc.
The children in the circle move towards the centre and endeavour to pat the 'dog'.

66 If you're happy and you know it

No equipment needed.

This game may be adapted to suit all ages. Simply adjust the actions and the words to fit the ability of the children in your group.

Children stand in a circle and follow the actions and word of the leader. Give individuals in the group the opportunity to choose their own words and actions. The basic verse is:

If you're happy and you know it,
Clap your hands!
If you're happy and you know it,
Clap your hands!
If you're happy and you know it,
Then you'll surely want to show it!
If you're happy and you know it,
Clap your hands!

Alternative ideas for younger children could include 'Touch your head', 'Nod your head', 'Touch your ears', 'Stamp your feet' and 'Swing your arms'.

Actions for slightly older children may be more adventurous and could include 'Jump up high', 'Sit on the floor', 'Hop on one leg', 'Wink with one eye', and 'Lie down and roll over' (bit of a mouthful but great fun).

67 Here is the beehive

No equipment needed

Here is the beehive *(hold up clenched hand)*,
but where are the bees?
Hiding away where nobody sees.
Now they come creeping out of the hive,
One, two, three, four, five *(straighten fingers one at a time)*
And away they fly *(flying movement with fingers)*,
up in the sky.
Buzz, buzz, buzz, buzz, buzz.

68 Here we come Loopy Loo

No equipment needed

The children dance round in a circle singing. They do the various actions as they sing the words:

> Here we come Loopy Loo,
> Here we come Loopy Lay,
> Here we come Loopy Loo,
> All on a Saturday night.
>
> Put your right hand in,
> Put your right hand out,
> Put your right hand in,
> All on a Saturday night.
>
> Put your left hand in, etc.
> Put your left leg in, etc.
> Put your head in, etc.
> Put your whole body in, etc.

69 Here we go round the mulberrry bush (or the Christmas Tree, if it's that season)

No equipment needed

The children dance round in a circle, singing. They do the actions as they sing the words:

> Here we go round the mulberry bush,
>   The mulberry bush, the mulberry bush.
> Here we go round the mulberry bush,
>   On a cold and frosty morning.
>
> This is the way we clap our hands, etc.
> This is the way we stamp our feet, etc.
> This is the way we shake our heads, etc.

70 I Stamp my feet

No equipment needed

This rhyme is said with actions throughout:

> I stamp my feet and wriggle my toes
> And clap my hands as the music goes.
> I reach to the sky and touch the ground,
> Up and down to the music's sound.
> I rock to and fro the way the wind blows.
> It's time to go when the music goes.

> I bounce up and down like a bouncy ball,
> And then I stretch up and grow very tall.

71 Let's pretend

You will need:

> *A whistle or music which can be stopped easily, eg a cassette recording or someone playing an instrument*

This is a fun game that also helps to develop the imagination.
   The leader tells the children that when the whistle blows, or the music stops, he will call out a name. Everyone will then pretend to be that person or thing, and show it in their actions. Some examples are: dog, cat, frog, sheep, cow, train, motorbike, aeroplane, horse-rider, doctor, policeman, soldier.

72 Miss Polly had a dolly

No equipment needed

The leader acts out the story with some exaggerated movements, and the children follow the leader:
> Miss Polly had a dolly who was sick, sick, sick.
> So she phoned for the doctor to come quick, quick, quick.
> The doctor came with his bag and his hat.
> And he knocked on the door with a rat-a-tat-tat.
> He looked at the dolly and he shook his head.
> He said Miss Polly put her straight to bed.
> He wrote a prescription for a pill, pill, pill.
> And she soon got better from being ill, ill, ill
(clap hands six times).

73 Musical bumps

You will need:

Some lively music

The children dance around to the music. When it stops, they sit quickly on the floor. When all are seated, the music starts again and the children carry on dancing. This can be repeated several times.

74 Open, shut them

No equipment needed

The actions for this game apply to both hands throughout.

> Open, shut them, open, shut them, give a little clap.
> Open, shut them, open, shut them, put them in your lap.
> Creeping, creeping, gently creeping right up to your chin.
> Open wide your mouth and teeth and pop a finger in.
> Falling, falling, quickly falling right down to the ground.
> Pick them quickly up again, and turn them round and round.

75 Magic ball

You will need:

A large sponge ball

The leader throws the ball at the children. Anyone touched by the 'magic ball' joins the leader and tries to hit other children with the ball. The last child to be touched is declared the winner.

76 Pop goes the weasel

No equipment needed

Form the children into three or four small rings, with one child in the middle of each. One child remains outside the rings. The children all sing:

> Half a pound of tuppeny rice,
> Half a pound of treacle,
> That's the way the money goes
> Pop goes the weasel.

On the word 'Pop', the children inside the rings and the child outside have to run and try to get inside another ring. The slowest child to get into a ring is the 'outsider' and will stand outside a ring until the next turn.

After a time, swap the children who have been part of a ring with those inside them.

77 Ring a ring o' roses

No equipment needed

The children form a circle, holding hands, and dance round singing:

> Ring a ring o' roses,
> A pocket full of posies,
> A-tishoo, a-tishoo,
> We all fall down *(they all fall to the ground)*.

78 Spinning the hoop

You will need:

A small hoop

Ask the children to stand side by side in a line. The leader calls out the name of one child, at the same time starting to spin the hoop. That child must run and catch the hoop before it falls to the ground.

79 Stations

You will need:

A number of bean bags

Stations are marked by bean bags. The children run about the room. At a signal (eg a whistle) each child must find a 'station' to stand behind. The leader removes a bean bag each time, so that the children are gradually eliminated.

80 Squirrels

No equipment needed

Five little squirrels sitting in a tree *(hold up five fingers of right hand)*.
The first one said, 'What can I see?' *(indicate thumb with left hand)*.
The second one said, 'I see a gun' *(indicate first finger with left hand)*.
The third one said, 'Away let us run' *(indicate second finger with left hand)*.
The fourth one said, 'Let's hide in the shade' *(indicate third finger with left hand)*.
The fifth one said, 'I'm not afraid' *(indicate fourth*

finger with left hand).
But BANG goes the gun *(a loud clap)*,
and away they all run *(show them running away)*.

81 Train

No equipment needed

Here is the train line, and here is the train *(stretch out right arm for the track, left hand clenched for the train)*
Chuff, chuff, chuff, along the line *(place left hand in palm of right hand and move up to shoulder)*
And chuff, chuff, chuff, back again. *(move back again)*

82 Tommy thumb

No equipment needed

As they say the rhyme, the children must choose the correct finger (or thumb), hide their hands behind their backs, then bring them forward with the appropriate finger upright, and the remaining ones clenched. Go through with them which name fits which finger before beginning the game.

> Tommy Thumb, Tommy Thumb, where are you?
> Here I am, here I am! How do you do?
> Peter Pointer, Peter Pointer, where are you?
> Here I am, here I am! How do you do?
> Teddy Tall, Teddy Tall, where are you?
> Here I am, here I am! How do you do?
> Ruby Ring, Ruby Ring, where are you?
> Here I am, here I am! How do you do?
> Sammy Small, Sammy Small, where are you?
> Here I am, here I am! How do you do?

83 What's the time, Mr Wolf?

No equipment needed

A
The leader stands at one end of the game area (he is Mr Wolf), and the children at the opposite end. At a signal, the children approach Mr Wolf from their end. They say in unison, 'What's the time, Mr Wolf?' Mr Wolf replies, 'Eight o'clock' (or any other hour). This is repeated until Mr Wolf says, 'Dinner-time.' Then he chases the children and catches all he can before they reach their 'home'. The children who have been caught join Mr Wolf at the catching end, until they are all caught.

B
Make one side of the room 'home', and form the children into a circle around Mr Wolf. They should be just out of touching distance. Then, all together, the children call out, 'Are you ready, Mr Wolf?' Mr Wolf says something like, 'No, I've still got to put on my trousers', or 'No, I've still got to put on my waistcoat.' Whatever item of clothing is mentioned, Mr Wolf has to pretend to put it on. After being asked three or four times if he is ready, he might suddenly say, 'Ready now'. Then he rushes for the children. The children race for 'home'. Whoever is caught becomes the next Mr Wolf.

5 Games for junior children (6 to 11s)

84 Altitude test

No equipment needed

Divide players into two equal teams and nominate a leader for each team. The aim of the game is for a team to respond quickly to a given command. Points can be awarded for swiftness of response: the team with the most points is the winner. The team leader is responsible for getting the correct response to the command.

Here are some ideas for commands, but think up more variations before playing the game:

'Get in height order, in line, facing me.'

'Lie down side by side in a line, in age order.'

'Using only your team members (ie without props), get as many as possible of your team off the ground at once.'

'Between your team there must be exactly (no more and no less) six feet, four hands and one bottom touching the floor.'

85 Animals

You will need:

A scarf to use as a blindfold

This is another version of 'Blind Man's Buff'. All the players, except the 'blind man', station themselves in different parts of the room. The blindfolded player then feels his way around the room until he touches somebody. The player who is touched must immediately make the noise of an animal – a donkey, cat, dog, cow or pig – repeating it three times if the blind man asks him to. The blind man has to guess the name of his victim by the voice. If he is successful, the person named becomes the blind man; if he is unsuccessful, the blind man must release his prisoner and try again.

86 Beachcombers

You will need:

A variety of simple objects such as matchboxes, pieces of wool, empty cotton reels
Masking tape to mark boundary lines

The players are divided into two teams: the beachcombers and the waves. The playing area is divided by a half-way line. Two other lines, one at either end, mark the boundaries for the game. The Waves and Beachcombers line up behind their respective boundary lines. The items are scattered on the Beachcombers half of the playing area. On the command 'Go', the Beachcombers and the Waves rush out together: the Beachcombers try to collect the treasure, while the Waves try to tag them before they reach the safety of home. If caught, a Beachcomber is out. The game recommences and is played till all the Beachcombers are caught. The teams then reverse roles.

The game can be competitive if the objects are given point values. The team gaining the highest total is declared the winner.

87 Bean game

No equipment needed

This can be played by any number. The participants form a circle and rotate in a clockwise direction as various 'vegetable' commands are called out by a person in the centre, as follows:
'Runner beans' *(all run round)*.
'Broad beans' *(walk round with arms out wide, taking huge strides)*.
'Dwarf beans' *(walk round, crouching)*.
'String beans' *(skip round holding hands)*.
'Haricot beans *(hop round)*.
'Baked beans' *(all scatter –* anyone caught before reaching the edge of the hall or room is 'in the tin'. They have to stand in the centre and help to catch the next time round. The last person left is the winner*)*.

88 Birthday cake

You will need:

1 kg of flour
A pudding basin
A tray
A sweet
A knife

Prepare the 'cake' by pressing the flour into a basin. Turn the basin upside down carefully on to the tray, remove the basin and put a sweet on the top of the 'cake'. The children sit in a circle with the cake in the middle, and one by one, they are chosen to cut a slice of it. The slices should be very thin and should be taken from all sides of the cake so that a tower is left standing. The aim of the game is to cut the flour away from the cake without disturbing the sweet. The one whose cut causes the sweet to fall must pick the sweet out of the flour in his mouth without using his hands.

A variation on this game is to pass a blunt knife round the circle, to music. When the music stops, the child holding the knife cuts a slice from the cake.

89 Black and brown bears

You will need:

A number of unbreakable chairs.

Chairs are scattered about the room, according to the number of players. One child is the 'black bear', the rest are 'brown bears', and the chairs are trees. 'Black Bear' chases the 'brown bears', but they are safe when sitting on the trees. All players must circulate while the music plays; the chase begins when it stops.

- 35 -

90 Blind feeding

You will need:

> A table
> Two chairs
> Two tablespoons
> Two soup plates
> Two large handkerchiefs
> A fair quantity of custard, porridge, or jelly (or, best of all, a mixture of all three)
> Two scarves

If the tables do not have suitable washable surfaces, it is wise to cover them with plastic sheeting before the game commences.

The leader arranges the table and the players so that they sit facing each other across the narrow part of the table, and so that the audience has a side view of the table. The players are both blindfolded, and a large handkerchief is tucked under their chins. A plate of food is set in front of each one. Each player proceeds to feed the other by filling their spoon with the food and aiming it at the other's mouth, which should be kept wide open. Set a time limit for this game. It is at its best when the rival players know each other well.

Players should be warned against waving their spoons about too wildly during play, as this can result in broken teeth.

91 Blowing in the wind

You will need:

> Drinking straws
> Tissue paper cut into small squares to represent leaves
> Chalk or masking tape to mark out playing area

Mark out a circle approximately 1.5m in diameter on the playing surface, and divide it into four quarters. Into each quarter, place an equal amount of paper 'leaves'. Divide players into four teams and give each person a straw. Each team is given a quarter of the circle as home base. On the starting signal, the teams try to blow their leaves out of their territory into any other section of the circle. Set a time limit. The winning team is the one with the least amount of leaves in their home base at the end.

92 Blow line

You will need:

> Several 10 m lengths of string
> Paper cups

Make a hole in one of the cups and thread it onto the string. Prepare one of these per team.

Two players from each team hold the string taut while the rest line up in single file at the end of the string where the paper cup is located. At the start signal, the first of these players blows the cup to the end of the string, then brings it back by hand to the start line. The others then take their turn. The first team to complete the course wins the game.

93 Boat race

No equipment needed.

Designate a starting and finishing line. A 'boat' consists of eight to ten players squatting in a crouched position, one behind the other, each holding the shoulders of the person in front.

Facing the players is a 'cox' who stands and holds the hands of the front player. The boat moves forward by all the players springing together off both feet, the cox assisting by calling out the rhythm. The activity should be made competitive, one boat racing against two or three others. During the race, any boat which founders, ie breaks into two or more parts, is eliminated.

94 Bubbles

You will need:

A pot of bubbles and a bubble blower
A paper fan or newspaper for each team

On the starting signal, the elected bubble blower from each team blows one good sized bubble, and the first player tries to fan it across a given line. The team members take turns to do the same. The team with the greatest number of bubbles crossing the line is declared the winner. You will need to have someone at the finishing line to record the scores.

A fun variation on this game involves putting colouring into the bubble mixture and getting each team member to blow a bubble and pop it against a white paper background. Have a different piece of paper for each team, and count up how many bubbles were burst on the paper by the teams after a set time limit.

95 Bucket cricket

You will need:

Two plastic buckets
A shuttlecock
Two table-tennis bats
Masking tape or chalk to mark out a pitch

Mark out a rough cricket pitch of any length. The plastic buckets are a substitute for wickets. The batsman stands in front of his wicket and defends it with a table tennis bat. If the bowler succeeds in getting the shuttlecock into the bucket, the batsman is out. Other rules may be introduced by the leader to suit the players' age range and local conditions.

96 Cards in bucket

You will need:

Chalk or masking tape to mark out a circle
A bucket or tin
Packs of playing cards or coloured or marked cards

Mark out a circle approximately 8m in diameter, and place the bucket in the centre. Stand teams around the edge of the circle. Each team has a differently marked pack of cards to differentiate them from the others. Give each player in a team ten cards to flick into the bucket. Players must stay 4m distance away from it. Scores are kept and the team with the most points is the winner.

97 Celebrity mix 'n' match

You will need:

   Lots of slips of paper

Write the names of movie stars on some slips of paper, and on others write the titles of the films they are associated with. Mix the papers and distribute them equally among the players, until none are left. Players who have the names of the film stars must find their matching film, and vice versa. The person who has paired off his slips in the shortest time wins.

To vary this game, you may use footballers and their teams/countries, pop stars and their groups, or the first and last names of celebrities (according to the age group and interests of the players).

98 Centipede shuffle

team · lots of · game space

You will need:

   An old piece of carpet or a hessian sack for each team
   Masking tape or chalk to mark the lines
   The floor surface needs to be polished or smooth for this game
   Small, equally numbered teams sit cross-legged in lines. A sack or small piece of carpet approximately 1m in length is supplied to number one in the team.

The starting line is marked directly in front of the team leaders and the finishing line marked approximately 7 m ahead. Sitting on the carpet or sack, the players shuffle forward using their heels or hands until they reach the finishing line. They then run back to the next player with the sack, the next player shuffles forward, and so on until everyone has completed the centipede shuffle. The first team to finish the course is the winner.

99 Cinders' slipper

You will need:

   A small slipper or shoe

The players sit on the floor in a circle, with legs outstretched and toes touching in the middle. One player, Cinders, is sent out of the room while the slipper is given to someone in the circle. The idea is to keep the slipper moving, under the legs of the players.

Cinders enters and says, 'I've lost my slipper.' She stands outside the circle, and tries to find the slipper by pointing to one of the circle of players. After each guess, she does a slow 360 degree turn, with her eyes closed, and then tries again to find the slipper by pointing to another member of the circle. When Cinders correctly points to the person hiding the slipper they swap places, and the game commences again. It's a very old game but good fun.

100 Clang the bell

You will need:

   A hoop
   A handbell or similar object
   Some small balls and string

Suspend the bell in the hoop so that it is nearly at the centre. Each player takes turn to throw a ball through the hoop from a set distance away and clang the bell. Each ring of the bell is a point awarded to the individual.

101 Climbing through newspaper

more than 15 · messy

You will need:

   Plenty of large broadsheet newspapers
   For younger children, an adult demonstration prior to the race might be helpful.

Relay teams, of any number of players, line up at one end of a room. On the command 'Go', number one in each team rushes forward to the team's designated pile of papers, takes a page and tears a hole. He then attempts to pass through the hole: the snag is that he must not break the outside edge of the paper in doing so. If he does, he takes a new page and begins the process all over again. Having passed through the paper to the satisfaction of the referee (it's best to have one for each team), he rushes back to his team and touches hands with the next competitor, who repeats the sequence. The first team to complete the exercise successfully is the winner.

More hilarious, ridiculously funny and much more difficult is playing the game in pairs (although it might be necessary to slim for a month before the event)! An even more difficult variation is to make players play this game in pairs, back to back.

102 Don't kick the can

lots of space

You will need:

A tin can, milk bottle or similar object

Players join hands in a circle around the can and attempt to push or pull one another to touch it. Any person touching or knocking over the can is out. If any two players let go hands, they are also disqualified. The winner is the one who manages never to touch the can.

103 Jack Frost

lots of space, all-age, more than 15

No equipment needed

This is a hectic game. One player is designated 'Jack Frost', and the other children run around trying to avoid him. Whoever he touches 'freezes' and stands still. They can only be 'thawed' if touched by another player. Set a time limit, and record the number of 'frozen' players. When one game is over, choose another Jack Frost and play the game again.

104 Contortions

lots of space, all-age

No equipment needed

Players stand around the room. The leader calls out various parts of the body that must be put onto, or next to, a particular object. Each subsequent demand requires the players to get into more difficult and contorted positions. Anyone losing their balance is immediately counted out. The last survivor is the winner.

Some ideas for commands: elbow to wall, nose on floor, thumb on nose, nose on elbow. Vary them according to age and ability.

105 Deer stalking

You will need:

A scarf to use as a blindfold

A 'hunter' and a 'deer' are blindfolded and placed at opposite ends of a large table. Set a two minute time limit. The hunter makes a noise by clapping his hand on the table, while the deer tries to avoid the hunter. Both must keep their hands on the table as they walk around the table. If they make bodily contact, hands are removed from the table, and the hunter makes a grab at the deer who tries to escape. The deer wins if he escapes and loses if he is caught.

106 Defend the fort

lots of space

You will need:

A stool or wooden box for a target
A sponge or foam ball for a missile.

Players sit in a circle. The person chosen to defend the fort sits on the stool or box in the centre. The object is to hit any part of the fort while the defender seeks to block the missile. Confusion can be created by passing the missile round the circle until suddenly a player makes a shot at the target. If the shot hits the target, the thrower changes places with the defender. The game continues for a set time, or until everyone has had at least one shot.

107 Discus throw

lots of space

You will need:

Some cardboard discs or paper plates

Individuals or teams compete by throwing discs from behind a line. Team points can be accumulated for those who throw the furthest. To avoid disputes, write the throwers' names on the discs.

108 Dog and bone

team game *lots of space*

You will need:

A 'bone' made up of a roll of newspaper in a stocking

This game is a golden oldie. Two equal teams face each other, sitting on chairs. Number the teams from opposite ends to each other. Place the bone on the floor, midway between the two teams.

The leader calls out a number. Both players with that number bolt forward from their opposite ends of the line, try to snatch the bone and get back to their seat without being tagged by their opponent. (Skill and cunning can be employed as players try to throw their opponent off the scent by making pretend grabs at the bone.) Once the bone has been grabbed, a dash must be made for home.

Points are awarded each time the bone is taken back to base without the person being tagged. If a tag occurs, then no points are awarded. The tagged player resumes his seat and continues to play as a team member.

109 Downing doughnuts

team game *messy*

You will need:

A small ring doughnut for each player
A length of string about 8–10 m long for each team

Divide players into teams of about four or five, and thread the ring doughnuts onto each string. Two helpers for each team hold the lines of string taut.

The teams have to eat all the doughnuts on their string one by one, without using their hands. They line up at one end of the string and, with hands behind their backs, the first players run to the first doughnut on their team string and eat it. As soon as the doughnut is devoured, they run back to their team and number two goes, and so on. The team that finishes first is the winner. For each whole doughnut eaten the team is awarded three points. If any portion of doughnut lands on the floor, a point is deducted.

110 Dressing race

team game

You will need:

A basket or bag for each team, containing hat, scarf, trousers, jacket, night-dress or dress

The players form small teams of approximately five people. Place a basket of clothing a short distance from each team. The first player runs to the basket, puts on all the clothes, picks up the basket and races around the back of the team to replace the basket in its original position. He then takes off the clothes, puts them in the basket and runs back to his team to touch the second player, who does the same thing all over again. The first team to finish is the winner.

111 Duster hockey

team game, lots of space

You will need:

Two hockey sticks or walking-sticks with rounded tops
Dusters or old socks made into a ball
Four chairs

Two teams face each other, sitting on chairs in a row or standing behind a line, as far away from each other as possible. Number the team members from opposite ends. Place the sticks and the 'ball' midway between the teams, and two chairs at either end to act as goal-posts. The umpire calls a number, and the two players with that number rush out, pick up a stick and attempt to score by hitting the ball into their respective goals. When a goal is scored, the equipment is put back in the centre, and the umpire calls another number. Players must keep the sticks below knee level.

112 Easy! Easy!

You will need:

A rope 6 m long

Two players sit cross-legged, facing each other approximately 6 m apart. Each holds one end of the rope. On a given signal, the players pull or slacken the rope, attempting to make their opponent topple over. The combatant who falls over first is eliminated.

In single combat games of this type, it is wise to play by the best two out of three falls. Otherwise, those who are slow to catch on will be at a disadvantage.

113 Elastic bands

You will need:

A large elastic band for each player

Each player puts an elastic band over his face so that it comes just beneath his nose and ears. The idea of the game is to wriggle the face until the band ends up underneath the chin. This may be played as a team game, with the band being passed down the team.

A variation on this game would be to use a tubigrip leg injury support. The player pulls a tubigrip over his head and down to his eyebrows. He then wriggles his face and forehead until the band comes off the top of the head. The player whose tubigrip pops off first is the winner. This can be played as a team game, with the tubigrip being passed down the team.

114 Escape ball

lots of space

You will need:

A football

Players form a circle, standing with legs apart, feet touching the foot of the person on either side of them. One player is chosen to be the first 'hitter' and stands in the middle of the circle. Using her hands only, she attempts to hit the ball through the legs of someone in the circle. Players can stop the ball with their hands only; no kicking is allowed. When the ball escapes the circle, the player through whose straddled legs it passed becomes the next hitter.

115 Farmyard frolic

lots of space

You will need:

Buttons or wrapped sweets
A chair for each team

Scatter a large number of buttons or sweets around the venue before the players arrive. Divide them into teams of three, four or five, one of whom is elected leader. Assign the name of an animal to each team. The game begins with the team leaders sitting on chairs while their teams search for the buttons or sweets. When one is found, the finder stays rooted to the spot, making the sound of the team animal. The leader rushes to collect it, thus freeing the team member to search again. After ten minutes, or when most of the 'goodies' have been found, the team with the highest number of objects is declared the winner. An extra prize or points may be awarded to the team making the most original and lifelike animal noise.

116 Flapping the kipper

team game

You will need:

Two pieces of paper cut in the shape of a kipper
Two boxes
Two rolls of newspaper

The players form into teams and stand behind a line about 2 m from the boxes. These are placed on their sides with the open ends facing the team. The first team member uses a roll of newspaper to flap the kipper from behind the line into the box. He then brings the kipper back to the next member of the team. The team to finish first is the winner.

117 Follow the light

You will need:

A torch
A sheet
A bucket of water and a sponge

This game will need to be played inside so that lights can be dimmed in order for players to see the torchlight. Hang, or have two non participants hold, a large sheet so that its bottom edge touches the floor. Send all of the players except one outside the room and position yourself behind the sheet with the torch, the bucket of water and the sponge.

Explain to your helper that you are going to play a trick on the ones who have gone outside and ask them to usher the victims in, one by one. Dim the lights. When the first player comes in, hold the torch behind the sheet and explain that he must put his nose on the point of light on the sheet and follow the light as it moves. He may not remove his nose from the sheet and must concentrate on keeping his nose on the light. Move the torch around behind the sheet, slowly at first and then faster, so that he is really concentrating. Finally, quickly move the light (and his nose) up to the top of the sheet and off it. As his face appears at the top, surprise him with a wet sponge in the face.

He then sits and enjoys watching the next victim.

118 Four-Legged musical chairs

team game

You will need:

> One chair for each trio of players
> Music
> Scarves or cords to join three people at the ankles

Set the chairs out in the largest circle possible. Players are grouped in threes, their legs tied as if in a three-legged race. One of the three sits on a chair while the other two team players sit on their knees. When the music begins, the trios walk around the room behind the chairs. When the music stops, they rush to sit down. However, one chair is removed each time the music starts. The last trio to be seated each time is eliminated. The winners are those who are seated when only one chair remains.

119 Front and back races

team game

You will need:

> Two saucers
> Small objects, eg buttons, beans or balls for each team (try to have twice as many objects as there are members in each team)

The aim of the game is to get every player passing a number of objects at speed. Team co-ordination and concentration is essential as objects are passed individually and quickly.

Teams of equal numbers stand sideways in line. On the floor, by the leader of each team, are two saucers, one containing the twelve small objects, the other empty. On the starting signal, the leader picks up one object and passes it to the second in the team, who passes it to the third, and so on down the line. When the object reaches the last player, he begins to pass it back down the line behind his back. In the meantime, other objects continue to be passed down in front. When the leader receives the objects behind his back, he puts them into the second and previously empty saucer. He must also count them as they come back to him, so that the instant he knows that the last object is back and in the saucer, he can shout 'Up', to indicate that his team has completed the race.

The number of objects to be passed can be varied, but whenever possible there should be at least twice the number of objects as players in the team, so that every player will be involved in passing objects in both directions at the same time.

This game should be played not less than four times, starting from one end on two occasions, and from opposite ends the other two times.

120 Gladiators

team game over-11s

You will need:

> A 5x10 cm plank of wood or a bench
> Two wooden paddles approximately 1m long, well wrapped in foam rubber or ethafoam to give plenty of protection

Two teams of players compete, one by one, to push their rivals off the wooden plank. The game is played in pairs as in 'Uncrowning the Monarch' (page 53). The two opponents stand face to face on the plank, paddles in their right hand. They must keep their left hands placed behind their backs. On the starter's signal each attempts to push their opponent off the plank with the paddle. Contact may only be made between knee and shoulder height. Any other place of contact on the body penalises the player. Points are awarded to the team for each player they push off the plank.

121 Glove and hat race

team game

You will need:

A pair of large gloves and a hat for each team

This is a relay in which any number of teams can join in. Teams are divided into two equal groups. Group A line up behind a starting line and Group B behind the finishing line. On the signal, the first person in each team dons the hat and gloves and races to the finishing line. There he passes the clothes to the next team person who puts them on and races back up the course.

Referees must make sure that players put the gloves on properly, with all fingers fitted into the fingers of the gloves.

122 Grab a bag

You will need:

Beanbags or similar apparatus (one less beanbag than there are players)
Some music

Players form a big circle around the pile of beanbags. When the music begins, they move round in a clockwise direction. When it stops, they dash into the centre to grab a bag. Failure to secure a bag means the player is out and they must go to sit on the edge of the circle. One or more beanbags are removed each time, and the game continues until only one player is left in.

123 Grab the loot

You will need:

Two oversized dice, easily made from wood or sponge cut into 50mm blocks, painted black and marked with white dots
Chalk or masking tape to mark the playing area

Mark on the floor or table a defined area about 1m square. One player rolls the dice onto the playing area and simultaneously calls a number between two and twelve. If the dots on the dice correspond in total to the called number, everyone grabs for the dice. Each dice is worth one point to the player who succeeds in getting it.

The roller can speed up the throwing for maximum excitement. The first to gain thirteen points is the winner.

124 Group puzzles

You will need:

A large but simple jigsaw puzzle

Each guest receives a dozen or so jigsaw pieces as they arrive. The object is for each participant to rid themselves of their handful by interlocking them into the picture in their correct place. Use a firm table or the floor for the construction of the puzzle, as this game can become quite a hilarious scramble.

125 Gourmets' relay

team game   messy

You will need:

A tray of simple but identical foods for each team, eg biscuits, chocolate, crust of bread, a pickled onion, a small apple, etc

Relay teams stand behind the starting line. On the command 'Go', number one in each team races to the other end of the course, eats one piece of food completely (no pocketing), whistles the first two lines of a well-known tune and dashes back to the start.

The rest of the team follow, one by one, each eating one piece of food and whistling the next two lines of the tune.

126 Guess who!

team game

You will need:

*A white sheet
A strong light
A pen and paper for each team*

A white sheet is hung across the room and a light is shone from behind it. The players divide into two teams. Members of one team take it in turns to walk behind the sheet so that their shadows are thrown on to it. The opposing team sits in front, guessing who is going by. The shadow players must do all they can to disguise their silhouettes. After everyone in the first team has crossed behind the sheet at least twice, the teams swap round. At the end of the game, the team with the most correct guesses wins.

As a variation on this game, instead of guessing which of the opposite team is making the shadow, players can imitate well-known characters, acting out some of their distinctive features, while the other team guesses who they are meant to be.

127 Hand football

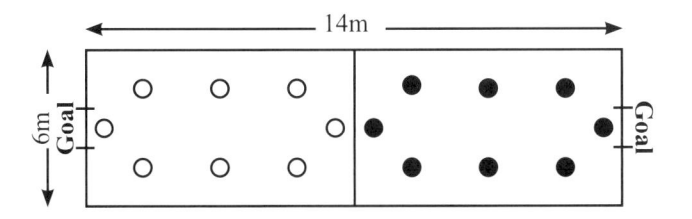

team game lots of space

You will need:

*A large rubber ball or football (though a small ball can be used)
Two skittles or tins, or chalk to mark the goal posts
The court is marked as shown in the diagram.*

All dimensions indicated in the diagram may be adapted and are largely dependent upon the playing area available. Similarly, the rules given below are for guidance only: they may be changed or modified to suit local conditions. It is suggested, however, that they should be kept as simple as possible.

- The object of the game is to score goals.
- The ball is propelled or knocked by the open hand or fist along the ground, and must always be kept below knee height.
- A ball which passes through the goal higher than knee height does not count as a goal.

128 Hidden halves

You will need:

A number of pieces of cardboard bearing the names of different towns and cut in half

When there are children of all ages at a party, this game may be adapted to suit the different age groups. The slips containing the second parts of the words should be hidden around the room or house, and the players given the first halves. They must find the slips which complete their half of a town. For younger children, the words can be split simply, so that they are easy to read, eg LON-DON instead of LO-NDON. Older children could be given the second half of the word and have to hunt for the first half.

As soon as player has completed his town, he takes both halves to the leader who gives him another half. The player to complete the most towns within a given time is the winner.

The game may be played with the names of flowers, advertising slogans, proverbs – there are many variations.

129 How many beans?

You will need:

*Small paper bags or envelopes
Dried peas or beans*

Each person is given the same number of beans in an envelope. They circulate around the room, offering one of their beans to anyone who can guess the number of beans in their closed hand. If anyone guesses incorrectly, she must hand over one of her beans. Set a time limit. The winner is the person with the most beans at the end of the game.

This can also be a useful 'icebreaker' game. The offerer might say, 'I'm (name). Guess how many beans I have in my hand.'

The person responds, 'I'm (name). You have … beans in your hand.'

130 Human obstacle course

lots of space

Children should be encouraged to wear suitable clothing for this energetic game

The obstacles are human beings and any number of obstacle postures may be adopted. For example:

'Kneelers' (on all fours, to go over or under).
'Straddlers' (going between outstretched legs).
'Poles' (standing erect, around which the others have to circle).
'Sitters' (with legs apart, to step in and among).

Competitors must not miss an obstacle or points will be deducted from the score.

The game may be played as a relay or as a competitive team game.

131 Human letters

more than 15, team game

You will need:

   Two sets of letters of the alphabet, large enough to be seen in a reasonably large hall
   A list of words (include every letter of the alphabet)

Divide players into two teams, giving each team a set of letters which they distribute among themselves. The teams line up opposite one another.

The leader shouts out a word from the list and the players holding the appropriate letters step one pace forward and arrange themselves in the order of the word. The first team to spell the word properly with the letters held up above their heads, scores a point. The chosen words should not contain repeated letters unless those letters are allowed for and extra cards made and distributed.

132 Javelin throw

You will need:

   Drinking straws, lightweight sticks or feathers

Players score points for accuracy as the 'javelins' are thrown at a target or over a line.

133 Moustache

You will need:

   A roll of electricians' plastic tape
   Some music (optional)

A group of players sit facing the rest of the group or audience. Each participant is given a 6cm strip of plastic tape which they apply to their upper lip. Using their facial muscles only, each person tries to remove the tape. The contortions are usually hilarious. The first person to be rid of his moustache is the winner and could be given a prize (with much ceremony) of a throw-away razor. Some background music often adds to the excitement.

134 Musical bizarre poses

lots of space

You will need;

   Live or recorded music

Players move around in time to the music. When the music stops, they freeze in whatever position they are in. Moving after the music has stopped means instant disqualification!

Players are then allowed to look round at each other, but anyone caught smiling or laughing at another person is out. The more eccentric the pose, the greater the fun. The game proceeds until one person remains, or the time is up.

135 Musical chaos

You will need:

One chair for each player

This game is like Musical Chairs, but more energetic. The chairs are arranged in a large circle (facing inwards). Instead of marching round the outside, the children charge about inside the circle until the music stops.

136 Musical couples

You will need:

A chair for every two players, minus one

Place chairs down the centre of the room, with every alternate one facing in the opposite direction. While the music plays, the players walk round the line of chairs in pairs. When the music stops each pair runs for a chair and both sit on it. The pair without a chair are out. Once they are moving again, a further chair is removed and the game continues until only one pair is left.

137 Musical mats

You will need:

One sheet of newspaper per player

The pieces of newspaper are placed on the ground. When the music stops, the last child to step on a 'mat' is out. The pieces of paper are removed one by one as the children are eliminated.

138 Paper ball fight

lots of space *messy* *team game*

You will need:

A large quantity of newspaper
Chalk or masking tape to mark a line

Two equal teams are separated by a row of chairs. Mark a line on both sides 1m from the barrier of chairs and give an equal amount of newspaper to each team.

The object of the game is for each team to make and throw as many paper balls as possible over the line of the opposing team, within a specified time. Team members can fend off the attackers' missiles so that they drop in 'No man's land'. Opponents' balls must not be thrown back. The penalty for this infringement is disqualification!

139 Passing the coins

team game

You will need:

Two 2p pieces

Two teams line up to face each other, with arms outstretched and fists clenched. The first player on the end of each team has a 2p piece placed on the back of one hand. On the command 'Go', they slide the coins from one hand to the other, and then on to the nearer hand of the next player, and so on up the line. Each coin must pass to the end without dropping. Should it fall, it is returned to the leader and the process set in motion again. The team completing the transfer in the approved manner is the winner.

Variations on this game include passing other objects, such as sugar cubes, sweets or chocolates. Similar passing games can be devised, eg passing tennis balls from under one chin to another, or hollow matchboxes from nose to nose.

140 Pictures and Puzzles

team game

You will need:

Pictures collected from old magazines, pasted onto cardboard and cut up

Divide players into two or more teams and distribute the jigsaw pieces among them. The teams have to try to complete a picture. Pieces may be swapped among teams on a one for one exchange rate. The team to complete their picture first wins the game.

141 Pig to market

lots of space — team game

You will need:

Empty milk or pop bottles
Brooms or walking sticks, one per team.

This can be played as a relay race in teams.

The idea is to push the bottle or 'pig' over a given distance to the finishing line, using the stick. The game is made more fun if two or three obstacles are set out on the course, which the 'pig' must go round or through.

142 Pigeon and eagle

lots of space

No equipment needed

This game originated in Bolivia. One player is chosen to be the eagle; another is chosen to be the pigeon. All the others form a circle and join hands. The eagle chases the pigeon around the circle. Those who make up the circle are on the side of the pigeon and let her pass freely under their clasped hands, but they try not to let the eagle come through. Set a time limit for each pair.

143 Posing

team game

No equipment needed

Divide players into two or more teams.

The leader announces that he is a film director in need of characters for his crowd scenes – He may opt for animals or people. He then calls out a phrase to describe the pose he requires, eg 'Kneeling Camels', 'Swinging Monkeys', or 'Saluting Soldiers'. The players must immediately freeze in that position, with appropriate facial expressions. The team which freezes first is awarded points. Alternatively a panel of judges can choose the best individual pose or the most realistic-looking team. Other possibilities include: the most ridiculous clown, the most frightening policeman, the saddest snail, the most spectacular goalkeeper.

144 Rhythm band

No equipment required

This is a non-competitive, robust game, but it does require some concentration from the players. Groups of four, six or eight players pair off. Each pair in the group is numbered so, for example, in a group of six there will be pairs 1, 2 and 3.

The leader sets the pace and speed according to the ability of the group. First, the group practises a rhythm of one beat per clap. Then they practise rhythms of two claps (marchtime), three claps (waltz time), four claps (common time) and so on. Once the basic rhythm is achieved, introduce more ideas to increase the fun:

- Clap the thighs.
- Clap above the head.
- Clap your right hand to your partner's right hand.
- Clap your left hand to your partner's left hand.
- Clap behind the back.

Once a pattern is established, further variations are possible as each group 'plays' a sequence of clapping actions in a continuous round. For example, the first group begins by clapping hands on their thighs in rhythm as practised. As Group 1 is on the second part of the sequence (clapping above their heads), Group 2 begins clapping the first part, and so on, until all the groups are participating. With a little practice, it's easier than it sounds!

For a really spectacular visual version, attach a half-metre of coloured ribbon to each player's wrist.

145 Roll up

You will need:

A quantity of identically sized marbles
A small bucket, tumbler or tin can

Players sit in a row and, one after another, bowl their marbles into the bucket, which is lying on its side. Each marble landing inside scores a goal, and the highest number of goals wins. This may also be played as a team contest between two sides.

146 Sale bargains

lots of space

No equipment needed

Four corners or areas of the venue are designated as shops, eg toy shop, chemist, bakery, greengrocer. All players assemble in the middle of the room. The leader calls out a commodity found in one of the shops, and players must rush to that shop. The last person to reach the shop is out. Players who go to the wrong shop are also counted out.

The winner of the last round, in which there will be two remaining competitors, is the person reaching the correct destination first.

147 Shipwreck

lots of space

You will need:

Labels for parts of a ship

Various parts of the room or playing space are labelled as parts of a ship (eg deck, lifeboat, bridge, captain's cabin). The players march round the middle of the room, until there is a shout of 'On deck!' or 'To the lifeboats!' The last one arriving in the correct zone is out, presumed drowned.

148 Shopping

You will need:

Four 'shops', each bearing a placard describing a selection of wares
Slips of paper with names of commodities
Counters and beans

Four 'shops' are set up, each bearing a placard describing its wares (eg, butter, toys, shoes). Each child is given a slip of paper with a commodity named on it (eg a pair of shoes). The children must take their slips to the correct shop, receiving a counter or a bean in exchange. On showing this to the leader, they are given another slip of paper, and so on. The winner is the one with the most counters at the end of the game.

149 Small box stack

You will need:

Small boxes, about five or six to each pair

Pairs compete to stack boxes in a vertical column. However, there is one handicap: they are not allowed to use their hands. The first team to complete their tower are the winners.

150 Speedway

more than 15 *team game*

No equipment needed

Several groups of players, ideally ten to fifteen per team, sit in close circles. One person is chosen to be the 'starter' in each group. On the command 'Race', the starter leaps up and yells 'Zoom!' The next group member immediately follows suit, and so on round the circle to complete a lap. As soon as a lap is completed, the whole team jump and yell, 'Lap completed, we're the greatest!'

The full race may demand three, five or even eight circuits. In the event of a multiple lap race, it is usually best to provide an independent marshal for each team.

151 Skittle ball

more than 15, lots of space

You will need:

A skittle or similar object
Two footballs in cardboard boxes

Two teams sit, facing each other. The players in each are assigned numbers. The skittle is placed midway between the two teams. The two balls, in boxes, are placed at the head of each team. When their number is called, the players with that number rush for the balls. Then, from behind their team, they throw the ball in an attempt to knock over the skittle. They continue throwing until one is successful or they exceed a previously agreed time limit (eg 30 seconds). The game continues until all the players have had at least one turn.

152 Story mime

No equipment needed

You will need a story containing a variety of animals or birds. Your own story with local characters mentioned will enhance the fun.

Sit the children in a circle with space between them. As the story is told, they have to imitate, both with actions and sounds, the birds or animals as they are mentioned. (Depending on the group you are playing the game with, you may want to create a rule that the last person to commence the mime each time a bird or animal is mentioned, is counted out of the game.) The story needs plenty of preparation to ensure variation, and maximum action from soaring eagles to the grovelling slimy grass snake which will take players from waving their arms high in the air to lying on their stomachs on the floor.

An idea for a story

I went for a walk in my garden this morning and heard two blackbirds singing (whistle or make bird noises). Suddenly onto the bird table alighted a large golden eagle (flying action) who, catching sight of me, immediately took off with a great flourish, soaring into the sky (arms furiously flapping). As I looked down at the path, I noticed that worms were crawling around (lie face down and wriggle on the floor). On my right three thrushes swooped (action) to catch the worms (action) as they struggled to reach the safety of their holes in the brown earth. From behind the rocks two prancing frogs (squatting and jumping) came through the long grass. Blue tits wiggled their heads from side to side (heads moving quickly from side to side) as they peered out (hands formed like binoculars around the eyes) of their nest in the garden shed. They were surprised to see the glistening frogs jumping in the sun (leap in the air) and they flew down onto the bird table (arms flapping) to get a closer look. A rabbit (bounce around the room) darted across the lawn, swiftly followed by a kangaroo (huge leaps). Just then the house telephone began to ring ('ding a ling, ding a ling' several times) and I had to go into the house...

The story can be adapted to include items of local interest. The competitive element can be removed, especially for younger children.

153 Story time

You will need:

A good imagination, or a storybook

Participants are each allocated a character or object in a story (eg Robin Hood, Friar Tuck, the sheriff, the sheriff's horse, the river, the town walls). Every time their character or object is mentioned they stand up, spin round and sit down again. On the mention of some all-inclusive object (eg 'the Merry Men'), everybody has to stand up and spin round together.

154 Sumo Wrestling

You will need:

A piece of chalk to draw a circle 2–3 m in diameter

About a dozen players stand huddled in the circle. At a given signal, they all try to push others out while trying to remain inside the perimeter line themselves. Any player with any of his body outside the circle is out. The winner is the person who eliminates all the other contenders.

A variation on this game is to have two teams, one team huddled inside the circle and the other outside. At a given signal the team outside tries to pull their rivals out over the line.

155 Tagging the team

lots of space — team game

You will need:

A square of foam sponge approximately 30x30x10 cm, covered or painted red on one side and blue on the other
Some canes or objects to mark out a goal area

The players are divided into two teams, and each team is designated one of the two colours on the foam. They line up about 6m apart, facing each other. The leader throws the coloured foam into the air, and shouts out the colour which is facing upward when it lands. If the colour is red, then the reds turn and make a dash for the safety of their goal area. The blues run after them and try to tag them. If tagged, a player joins the opposing side. The game is restarted again and again until one side is eliminated, or the time limit expires. If playing to a time limit, the team with the most players at finishing time is declared the winner.

156 The sea and her children

lots of space

No equipment needed

All the children stand in a circle around one player who is the 'sea'. A leader calls out instructions and the children have to carry out the corresponding actions until a new command is called: 'The sea is choppy' (they jump); 'The sea is calm' (they walk); 'There are surfers on the sea' (mime people surfing).

When the leader says, 'There's a storm at sea, and the sea wants her children', they all try to run to the edge of the room, or to a designated 'base', before the sea catches them. Anyone who is tagged is out.

157 Tissue whirlwind

team game

You will need:

A box of medium tissues

Groups of six or more gather in tight circles and elect a leader. On the command 'Airborne', the group leader throws a single tissue into the air. Without touching the tissue with any part of the body, the group members attempt to keep it airborne by blowing. The group who keeps their tissue in the air for the longest time gains points. Four to six attempts need to be made to help players get used to the game and to perfect their team blowing technique.

158 Toeing

lots of space — team game

You will need:

Some lemons
A piece of chalk

Two teams compete to push a lemon along a clearly marked chalk line, approximately 12m long. The catch is that they must do this by sitting on their bottoms and pushing the lemon with their feet. One at a time, competitors shuffle on their bottoms along the line, guiding the lemon. On completing the course, each player picks up their lemon and rushes back to the beginning so that the next team member can start.

159 Treasure chest

You will need:

   A scarf, a bunch of keys or a baby's rattle or ball

The children sit in a circle, with one child in the middle. He is blindfolded and is guarding his 'treasure' (the scarf) which is placed on the ground in front of him. The leader quietly points at someone in the circle, who then creeps towards the treasure and attempts to take it without the blindfolded child hearing. If he hears a sound, he points towards the direction he thinks the sound is coming from. If he points in the right direction, the moving child must sit down, and the leader points at someone else who tries the same thing. If a child succeeds in taking the 'treasure', he takes the place of the blindfolded person.

160 Tutti-frutti

You will need:

   A chair for each player

All players sit on chairs in a circle. The leader goes round the circle designating each player as a fruit, eg banana, apple, grape, orange, date. When the leader calls out the name of a specific fruit, eg orange, all the oranges must change seats. The last person to find a seat is out and their chair is removed. Any combination may be called at the same time. If 'Fruit salad' is called, everyone has to change places.

161 Topple the king

team game

You will need:

   A good supply of old newspaper
   Two paper crowns

This is a good rousing game with plenty of spectator value.

   Two equal teams sit in a line opposite each other, at least 2 m apart, with their supply of newspaper. All players remain seated throughout the game. One team member from each side is elected king, and they wear the crowns. The others are knights.

   The object is to displace the crown of the opposing team's king by attacking it with paper ammunition, eg screwed up paper balls or paper airplanes. Teams may vary their tactics from single shots to a concerted organised barrage. The king cannot defend himself, but all the noble knights can use their hands to ward off missiles and retaliate, seeking to knock off the opposing king's crown.

   Each time the crown is removed, the opposing team gains a point.

162 Tramps' tea-party

messy

You will need:

   A knife and fork
   Scarf, gloves and an old hat
   A dice
   A loosely wrapped newspaper parcel, with a bar of chocolate in the middle of it

The players sit in a large circle, with the parcel in the centre on a table or on the floor. Each player throws the dice in turn. When a six is thrown, the thrower runs to the parcel, puts on all the clothes and begins undoing the parcel, using only the knife and fork. As soon as another player throws a six, he takes the clothes off the first player, puts them on himself and proceeds to continue unwrapping the parcel. When the wrapping is off the chocolate, players try to eat it, using the knife and fork.

   You can simplify (and shorten) this game by not wrapping the chocolate in paper.

163 Uncrowning the monarch

team game

You will need:

Newspaper to make simple hats

The players are divided into two even teams and numbered. They all stand in a circle, with two hats placed in the centre. The leader calls out a number, and the players with that number run into the centre, don a hat and attempt to dislodge their opponent's headgear while keeping their own on. They are only allowed to do this with their hands. No other kind of bodily contact, eg pushing or shoving, is allowed. When one succeeds, they replace the hats and return to the circle.

164 Wrapping the team

messy team game

You will need:

A supply of toilet rolls for each team

Divide players into two teams. Members line up, one behind the other, with their legs apart. Both teams are given an equal number of toilet rolls. The first team member picks up a toilet roll, and unrolls it over his head to the next person, who unrolls it, passing it on to the next, and so on down the line to the last in the team. The roll is then passed through the legs back up to the first person in the team, who promptly repeats the process. When a roll runs out, another is joined to it: the leading team member has to pass this through his legs to the person making the join. The game proceeds until time is up and rolls envelop the entire team.

If a roll is dropped and rolls out of reach, the whole team must shuffle, without breaking their wrapping, into a position where one member can reach it and carry on wrapping the team.

6 Indoor games for young people

Leaders who introduce games to teenage groups get mixed reactions. Some young people feel too sophisticated to participate, while others enjoy joining in, what for them, is often a novel experience. One of the keys to success lies in knowing your group and selecting appropriate activities.

165 Alphabet ping pong

lots of space

You will need:

Some table tennis balls
Hardback old books or pieces of hardboard (approx 15x25 cm), one for each player

Players stand in a circle, holding the book or board in both hands to use as a bat. Someone starts the game by batting the ball to another player while calling out the letter 'A'. The receiver bats it to someone else calling 'B', and so forth. The team works together to see how far down the alphabet it can get before the ball touches the ground.

This may be used as a competitive game, with several teams having a go.

166 Are you...?

You will need:

A list of famous couples, eg Romeo and Juliet, Anthony and Cleopatra, Tom and Jerry
A booby prize

Write each name on a separate slip of paper, fold the slip in half and place it in a box. Give the box a good shake.

Players sit in a circle and each is handed a name which he keeps hidden from the others. Each player in turn is then allowed to ask one question of anyone else in the circle, trying to identify their partner. They cannot ask a direct question, however, such as, 'Are you Cleopatra?' until they are fairly certain of the other's identity. The first to challenge correctly is the winner, and he and his partner drop out of the circle. The game continues until only two are left, and they are awarded a booby prize.

167 Art gallery

You will need:

 A pile of old newspapers
 A small prize

At the beginning of the game, newspapers are distributed to everyone. The leader then calls out an object, eg a bunch of bananas, a string of sausages, a horse, a rabbit, a church building. The players have to tear out the appropriate shape. The game is continued for several items, and an 'art gallery' of exhibits arranged at the end. The player producing the best array is awarded a small prize.

168 Ascot bonnet

You will need:

 Several pairs of discarded nylon stockings or football socks
 A supply of ladies' head scarves and some large man-size gloves
 All shoes need to be removed before the game commences.

The players divide into two teams and stand in rows, facing inward. Number one in line puts on the gloves, pulls on the stockings up to the knee, then covers his head with the scarf and ties it under the chin. Number two in each team pulls off the gloves, stockings and scarf, and dons them in similar manner. All the other players follow suit. The last person in the team to complete the procedure throws the gloves, stockings and scarf in the air, shouting, 'Jumble sale!'

169 Associated numbers

No equipment needed

Players sit facing the leader who calls out a number and points to a player. The selected player must immediately respond by shouting back an associated word or phrase. Failure to respond is counted as a life lost - three lives lost and the player is out.
 Examples of association:
 4 Seasons or Gospels
 10 Commandments
 2 is company, three's a crowd
 9 lives of a cat

170 Banana race

messy

You will need:

 A banana for each competitor

Each player is given a banana. On the signal 'go' all players try to peel and eat their banana while holding one hand behind their back. The first to finish and whistle 'God save the Queen', or some other chosen song, is the winner.

171 Changing places

lots of space

You will need:

 One chair per person

The chairs are arranged in a circle, facing inwards, with one player sitting on each chair. The object of the game is to whittle down the number of players. The leader will need two helpers to remove the chairs as the game proceeds.
 The leader calls for certain players to move, eg 'All those wearing blue change places'. (Prepare a list beforehand, so that the game keeps moving at a reasonable pace.) While the players are moving, the two helpers remove one or two chairs according to the number of participants.
 Examples of commands could be 'Those wearing red socks', 'Those with blonde hair', 'Those wearing earrings', or 'Those wearing size 7 shoes'. To get everyone involved, have an occasional request which will necessitate that all the players move, eg 'All those wearing shoes', or 'All those with a nose' or 'All those with two ears'.

172 Charades

team game

No equipment needed:

A popular 'golden oldie'. Players are divided into small groups of five or six. In a private huddle, each group selects a word of two or more syllables which they act out as a group in front of the other teams. After a few minutes' thinking time and collaboration each syllable is acted out in pantomime, then the whole word must be incorporated into the final act. The first spectator team to give the correct answer is awarded points and they, in turn, act their charade.

The following will illustrate how to act out the syllables:

Titanic: Tie (putting on a tie)… tan (sunbathing, someone pointing to a tan) … nic (someone removing an object from another person's pocket)

Slapstick: Slap … stick

Infancy: Inn …. fan …. sea

Robinson-Crusoe: Rob …. inn …. son…. crew …. sew

Situation: Sit …. chew …. way …. shun

173 Chinese laundry

team game

No equipment needed:

Divide the players into four equal groups, and place one group in each corner of the room. Appoint a captain for each group. The leader stands in the centre of the room and calls out the names of the articles he lost when he sent his washing to the laundry. When an article is named, eg a grey sock, a white left trainer, a hairclip, a bunch of keys, each team tries to find one. It is taken out (or off) and given to the team captain, who runs with it to the leader. The first team to reach the leader with the correct item wins the point.

174 County count

team game

You will need:

A blank map of England, or a country of choice, with counties clearly marked
A pencil for each team

Prepare beforehand a list of well-known towns and places of famous historical interest in the counties or countries on the maps. The object of the game is to locate the names in the appropriate county and in approximately the correct area. Divide the players into small groups of three or four.

The leader reads the list of places one at a time, giving time for the players to confer and write where they think it is on their map. The map judged to be the most accurate at the end is the winner.

175 Detection search

You will need:

A number of miscellaneous small objects (see below)
A list of each item
Pencils and paper for each player

The objects are secretly and discreetly given to each player as they arrive. They are warned not to talk about the game. Every player places the object on his person so that it can be seen but it must be camouflaged. So, for example, a pencil could be sticking out of a coat pocket, a pin upside down on a coat or dress, or a piece of wool attached to a jumper.

At a given signal, the players search for the articles using their eyes only. When they find them, they note down the object, together with the name of the person and a description of where it was hidden on them. When someone has completed the full number of items (players need to be told beforehand how many items they are looking for), his list is checked privately while the game continues. The first completely accurate list is the winner.

Set a time limit to shorten the game, and make the player with the largest number of correct entries at the end, the chief detective. A pair of toy handcuffs or a large badge could be awarded as a prize.

The leader should remember:
- To know where the objects are hidden and the

name of the player bearing each item
- To announce at the beginning the number of items to be found
- To remind players that only eyes may be used to discover the objects, not hands

The game becomes hilarious as each individual tries to achieve the maximum number of inspections.
   Some suggestions for camouflaged objects:
   A piece of Sellotape stuck on a collar
   A postage stamp on a dress
   Cotton wound round string of beads
   A blob of silver paper on a tie clip or brooch
   A hairpin in hair
   An extra button on a coat
   A brown shoelace in a black shoe
   A small paper clip on a coat pocket flap.

176 Double blow line

team game

You will need :

   String cut in 10 m lengths
   Plastic or paper cups

Tape two cups together, bottom to bottom. Pierce a hole through the bottoms and thread them onto a string. The game is played in teams of four persons. One player from each team holds the line straight and taut. The cups are placed in the centre of the string. On the signal for battle to begin, the remaining two players for each team stand one each side of the string and try to blow the cups to their opponents' end. A goal is scored when the cup reaches the hand of the string holder.

177 Drink and blow

team game

You will need:

   Two candles and sticks
   Two boxes of matches
   Water and drinking cups

Form two teams of five to seven players.
   Place the two candles 15 cm apart on a table, with matches to hand. Two players sit opposite their team's candle, and a glass of water is placed in front of each candle. In turn players light their candle and try to drink their cup of water, while the opposite player tries to blow out the candle. The game has good spectator value as competitors have the dilemma of deciding whether to drink, protect their candle, blow out their opponent's candle or relight their own. A good referee is essential.

178 Duck fighting

lots of space

No equipment needed

Players crouch in pairs, as shown. Keeping still themselves, they try to make their opponent lose balance by pushing with their hands. This is a static balance activity which can be made dynamic by allowing the pairs to hop or spring about while trying to unbalance each other.

179 Electric fence

team game

You will need:

A string tied between two chairs at about 30 cm height
This game should be played on a soft, carpeted floor.

Form two teams of players roughly equal in size. The task is to get the whole team over the 'electric fence' without getting electrocuted by touching the fence. Each team takes it in turn: first one person from one team gets over, then one from the other team. Players may receive help from their team members, but once they are over they cannot assist their team in any way. The last member has to cross without any assistance. When both teams have negotiated the fence, the string is raised a little and another round is played. The fence is raised after each round, as in the high jump.

One member touching the fence eliminates his whole team. (You may decide, however, that three or four 'touches' from any team should be the elimination figure.)

180 Exchange and credit

You will need:

Coloured paper in eight or ten different shades

In advance, prepare one set of 2 cm paper squares for each player. Each set contains the same number of squares (about 8–10), each square is a different colour with the same combination of colours in a set. Determine a value for each colour – green may be worth 2 points, red 10 points, yellow 5 points, and so on. Make up clues to help players guess at the values of the paper squares, eg 'Yellow is worth more than green', 'Red is twice the value of yellow'.

Set a time limit in which to play. Instruct the players to begin exchanging the pieces of paper according to their own estimate of what they are worth. Introduce the clues at intervals during the game. After a period of play, stop the game, give the values for each paper square and find out who has the most points.

181 Feather football

team game

You will need:

Two or three feathers

Mark out a small pitch. Two teams of not more than two or three players compete to blow a feather over the opposing team's goal-line.

This game may be played on a floor or a large table. You may need to set a time limit.

182 Find the route

team game

You will need :

A small supply of local bus and rail timetables

Sort out beforehand half a dozen difficult but not impossible journeys, including plenty of changes and with plenty of possible alternatives. Divide the players into teams, give them a timetable each, and tell them that you are planning a pretend journey. Tell them that you have certain time restrictions and set them the challenge of finding your route. For example the challenge might be for them to find a way from Little End to Battersborne in less than two hours on a Saturday evening after seven o'clock. The first team to find the route is the winner.

183 Food trivia

You will need:

*Sheets listing the quiz questions below, or blank pieces of paper
Pencils*

Give each player a paper and set a time limit. The first person to complete the quiz correctly (or as nearly as possible) is the winner.

1. Does an ounce of milk chocolate contain approximately
   - (a) 150 calories
   - (b) 210 calories
   - (c) 75 calories

2. Which confectionery bar is advertised with the slogan 'Have a break, have a ....'

3. How much chocolate do American citizens consume in an average year?
   - (a) 2 million pounds
   - (b) 2 billion pounds
   - (c) 4.5 million pounds

4. In a box of 100 Smarties what colour is the favourite?
   - (a) Red
   - (b) Green
   - (c) Brown

5. How many calories are there on average in a 170g portion of fried beef steak?
   - (a) 210
   - (b) 475
   - (c) 150

6. Which of the following vegetables has the least calories in a 113 g cooked portion?
   - (a) Cabbage
   - (b) Cauliflower
   - (c) Broccoli

7. How many people world-wide earn their livelihood from Coca-Cola?
   - (a) approximately 5,000
   - (b) approximately 1 million
   - (c) approximately 7,500,000

8. How many cans or bottles of Coke do you think are consumed each day?
   - (a) 100,000
   - (b) 6 million
   - (c) 601 million

Answers
1. (a).
2. Kit Kat.
3. (b) 2 billion, according to the Chocolate Manufacturers' Association of the USA.
4. (c) Brown.
5. (b) 475 calories.
6. (a) cabbage = 10 calories, cauliflower = 12 calories, broccoli = 16 calories.
7. (b) 1 million.
8. (c) 601 million.

184 Getting acquainted

No equipment needed

Form groups of five or less. Each person gives four facts about themselves concerning their home, their family, their school and their hobbies. Three of these facts must be true, one a complete lie! The others then have to guess which was a lie. You will really learn a lot about your group in a short time.

Award points to the individual who spots the lie. The person with the highest score after hearing everybody's facts is the winner in each group. The group winners then demonstrate their 'lie detection skills' by forming a group and playing another round to find the champion lie detector among them.

185 Getting to know all about you

No equipment needed

This game is played in groups of no more than ten or twelve players, and is a great 'ice-breaker'.

Each group sits in a circle. One person starts the game by announcing his name and a 'made up' description of himself in rhyme. For example:

'I am Fred, I love my bed.'
'I am John, I come from Canton.'
'I am Jane, I live in Spain.'
'I am Tom, the Piper's son.'

The next person repeats what the first said, and then adds his name and description. The next person repeats the previous two names and rhymes, and adds his own. It gets tougher on the memory as the game proceeds, but this keeps everyone alert.

This can be a competitive game, with the winner being the first person to repeat what has been related by all the members of the circle.

For fairness and accuracy, it might be as well for someone to write down each individual's contribution as it is originally given.

186 Getting to know you

You will need:

A ball of string

Players sit in a circle. The first player holds the ball of string and introduces himself in two minutes or less, giving his name, job/school, interests, hobbies, etc. Holding the end of the string, he then throws the ball of string across the circle to another player, preferably someone not known to him, and that person introduces herself to the group. Players hold on to the string for the duration of the game. The game continues so that as many participants as possible have an opportunity of sharing. The game ends when the string runs out, or an agreed time is completed.

The string criss-crossing is a symbol of friendship and linking together.

187 Gossiping

You will need:

Two concentric circles of chairs – the inner circle facing inward, the outer circle outward
Music

Players form two equal groups, one occupying the outer circle, the other the inner circle. When the music starts everyone rises and the inner group walks around the inner circle in a clockwise direction, while the outer group walks round the outer circle anti-clockwise.

When the music stops, each player faces the person opposite and, in a few short sentences, they discuss a topic set by the leader.
- My most embarrassing moment
- My favourite food at MacDonalds and the reason I like it
- The sport I would like to see included in the Olympics
- The country I would most like to visit, and why
- The qualities I like most in a person
- My favourite programme on TV, and why
- My least favourite kind of music
- Some of the best moments in my life so far

188 Grape toss

messy team game

You will need :

Plenty of seedless grapes or small marshmallows

Do not play this game on an expensively carpeted floor!

Place an equal number of grapes in bags and give one bag to each team. Divide into teams of four or five. The teams form circles, by holding hands initially so that the circles are more or less the same size. Each team appoints a grape-tosser, who stands in the centre of the circle holding a bag of grapes. On a given signal, he tosses a grape to each team member in turn, who must catch it in their mouth. No hands are allowed! Points are given for each grape successfully caught. The penalty for each grape dropped is one point deducted from the score. The game continues round the circle until the grapes are finished. The winner is the team with the highest score.

189 Hand wrestle

No equipment needed

Two players face each other, each holding the other's right hand, the outer edges of their right feet together. They brace themselves. At a signal, one tries to throw the other off balance. As soon as either foot is moved, a point is given for the person whose feet remain stationary.

This can be a competitive team game. Set a time limit for each pair.

190 Handicap snatch

lots of space *team game*

You will need:

One 'hay' bag – a plastic or cloth bag filled with lightweight material

Two equal lines of players face each other 7–10 m apart – these are the horses. Behind each line of horses are another two equal lines – the jockeys, each of whom is partnered with a 'horse'. Each team member is numbered. When a number is called out, those jockeys mount their horses and move to the centre of the play area to snatch their hay bags. The aim is for the horses to get back to their line with the hay bag, jockey still mounted, without being tagged by the other jockey. Points are awarded for each horse that gets back safely. If someone is tagged, however, no points are awarded.

Jockeys cannot mount until their number is called, and must keep their feet off the ground after that until they are safely home.

191 Happy families

You will need:

Sets of three cards depicting a family – give each family a different, silly name, eg Mr Blot, Mrs Blot and Baby Blot
An appropriate number of chairs

Set out groups of three chairs around the room, but have one group less than the number of 'families' taking part. Four other chairs are placed one in each corner of the room. Mix up the family cards, divide them into four piles, and put a pile on each of the corner chairs. The players gather together in the middle of the room. On the word 'Go', they rush to one of the corner chairs and grab a card. Immediately they start shouting out their 'family' name seeking to find the other members of their family. As soon as they have done so, the family rush to be seated on one of the groups of chairs. While all the shouting has been going on, the leader has removed one set of three chairs. The family left standing is out.

For the next round, the cards are quickly collected and replaced on the corner chairs. This time, the players move around the room, until a whistle blows or some other alerting sound is made. Everyone races to get a family card. However, there are now more cards on the four chairs than players, who may have to keep returning to the chairs to find another card before they can make up the family. The whole process is continuously repeated until only one family – the winners – are seated.

192 Head of the river

team game

You will need :

Large boxes, eg electric appliance and TV boxes (usually available from electrical goods suppliers)
Masking tape or chalk to mark a line for the river

Teams line up behind a starting line. The first player in each team places a box over her head, with the open end facing floorways. On the starting signal, she has to make a journey up and down the river, guided by her teammates, who shout their directions from behind the starting line. Being 'blind', there is usually lots of bumping on the 'boats'.

Each player has a turn. The first team to complete the course and stand in line behind the starting post is the winner.

It is a good idea to have a safety person walking any younger players down the course.

193 Horsemen, knights, Henry VIII

lots of space

You will need:

Background music (optional)

Players find a partner, and the pairs move around the room as the music plays. When the music stops, the leader calls out one of the following instructions:

When he cries 'Horsemen', one of the pair scrambles down on all fours like a horse and the other sits on him.

When he cries, 'Knights', one goes down on one knee and the other sits on his knee.

When he cries, 'Henry VIII', one jumps into the other's arms and is safe from the marauding king.

The leader may call the movements in any order. The last pair to form the position is out. The last pair in the game at the end are the winners.

194 Human noughts and crosses

team game

You will need:

Nine chairs

Form two teams, one 'Noughts' and the other 'Crosses'. Set out nine chairs in rows of three. The leader calls out, 'Noughts' and 'Crosses' alternately and, in turn, members of the teams go and sit on the chairs. The object is to get a row of three human 'Noughts' or 'Crosses', exactly as in the paper game. The team that gets a row of three takes a point but a draw counts to neither side. When each game is over, those who have played go to the end of their team, so that everyone is given a chance to play. As the team to take up the first position has the advantage, if a 'Nought' was called first on the first round, a 'Cross' should be called first on the second round.

195 Human scavenger hunt

lots of space team game

No equipment needed

Divide into teams and have each team choose a leader. All team members must stay within a prescribed playing area. A judge stands in a position equidistant from all teams. For example, if there are four teams, the teams can position themselves in the four corners of the room and the judge can stand in the middle.

The judge calls a characteristic similar to the ones listed below, and the leader on each team tries to locate someone on the team who fits the characteristic. As soon as someone is found, the leader grabs that person by the hand and both run to the judge. The first team leader to touch the hand of the judge wins points for the team.

Someone wearing glasses
Someone with blue eyes
Someone who exercises regularly
Someone who enjoys ice cream
Someone who loves cabbage
Someone wearing jeans
Someone wearing aftershave or perfume
Someone who plucks her eyebrows

Make up your own list with your group of players in mind.

196 Human spelling

more than 15 team game

No equipment needed

For two teams of players, with not less than twenty in each group. The teams stand in lines, holding hands. The leader calls out a word and the team members have to spell it, using their bodies and by lying on the floor. The first team to spell a recognisable word gains points. The words you choose will be determined by the number of players in the group.

197 Introductions

You will need:

Ten matchsticks for each player

Give each player ten matchsticks. A player takes a number of matchsticks in one hand and holds out his clenched fist to another player, demanding, 'odd or even?' The other player gives his answer and, if he has guessed correctly, the person holding the matchsticks hands one of them over. His opponent then goes through the same routine with some of his own matches. If the original questioner guesses incorrectly he hands over another match. However, if his guess is correct, he collects a match from his opponent.

When the time is up, the player with the greatest number of matchsticks is the winner.

198 Japanese wrestling scrum

You will need:

A doormat, or similar

This is an energetic game and must be well supervised.

Players stand in a circle around a mat, holding hands. On the command 'Commence battle', they pull, push or in any way try to get members of the circle to touch the mat without stepping on it themselves. Once a player has touched the mat, they are out. The only other penalty is if the circle breaks: the two players who let go are eliminated.

199 Knight's combat

You will need:

A soft playing surface, eg carpet or mat

Definitely a rough game, but great fun! Players are in pairs, one riding piggyback – the knight on his horse. The combat between two pairs is won when one knight is tumbled to the floor or dismounted.

The winning pair can challenge others, or the game may be played as a team game.

200 Lace up

more than 15 *team game*

No equipment needed

Players form groups of ten to fifteen and stand in circles. Everyone takes off their shoes and piles them in the centre of their circle. On the word 'go', the group moves away to another pile of shoes nearby. On 'go two' they tie all the shoelaces together in knots. On 'go three', they pick up the pile and deposit the shoes in another part of the field/hall. On 'go four' everyone runs for their own shoes. The first team back with all their shoes on and laced up wins.

201 Learning DIY

team game

You will need:

A large supply of buttons
Plenty of pieces of cloth,
Reels of cotton
Needles
Some stout pieces of wood approximately 450x150x45 mm
Packets of tacks and a hammer for half the number of players

Divide into two teams. Give one team the buttons, cloth, needles and cotton. Give the other team the wood, tacks and hammers. The aim is to sew on as many buttons and hammer in (straight!) the greatest number of tacks within a given time. At half time the teams swap tasks and are given new supplies of basic materials. The team to complete the greatest number of tasks in each half are the winners.

202 Long John stuff

lots of space *team game*

You will need:

Two pairs of large long johns or tights
About fifty small balloons

Divide players into two teams. Each team selects their 'Long John' who puts on the garment over their regular clothes. Elect two players in team to be 'stuffers'. Give each team an equal number of balloons. The object is to get as many of them inside the 'Long Johns' as possible, within a specified time.

The teams line up approximately 10m from their 'Long John' and 'stuffers'. On the signal, they have to blow up and tie balloons, then, one by one, run to the 'stuffers' who promptly stuff 'Long John'.

Much can be made of a ceremonial countdown as a judge pops, with care, each balloon while the team counts loudly.

203 Milko

messy *team game*

You will need:

Two chairs
Rubber gloves
Two aprons
Water and two buckets

Divide players into two teams.

Make small holes in each finger of the rubber gloves, fill them with water, and hang them from a chair, over a bucket. Set a time limit. On a whistle blast, each player in turn rushes to don the apron and milk the 'cow' into the bucket. The first team to milk the 'cow' dry is the winner.

Caution! Have additional rubber gloves and some absorbent floor covering in case of accidents.

204 Mime rhyme

No equipment needed

About six people are sent out of the room. The rest decide on a word which those outside have to act – but they actually give them a word that rhymes with it. Those outside come in and mime all the words they can think of that rhyme with the one they have been given. For example, if the word chosen is 'spark', and the players are told that it rhymes with 'lark'; they can mime 'mark', 'dark', etc, until they hit upon 'spark'.

205 Miming game

team game

No equipment needed

Divide players into teams of about six and send one team out of the room. Those remaining decide what they will ask the people outside to mime (one at a time), eg bathing a baby, making a cake, starting up a car after backing out of the garage. The first person comes in and is told what to act. The second comes in and watches their mime, and then copies what he has seen to the third to come in. This continues until everyone outside has come in. The last person has to guess what the previous people in his team have been miming. If possible, the first person should repeat his act for the benefit of the guesser and to the amusement of the rest.

206 Musical laps

You will need:

Enough chairs for half the number of players

This game is played on the same principle as Musical Chairs, except that half the children remain seated. The rest have to find a lap to sit on, instead of a chair, when the music stops.

207 One minute, please

You will need:

> Some slips of paper
> A hat

Sitting in a circle, the players each take a slip of paper out of the hat. Some will draw blanks; others will have a subject for a one-minute speech. They speak on their subject in turn, and their speeches are judged by the volume of applause from the audience.

Suggested topics: 'Dog collars'; 'Ladies hats'; 'The glories of Wales'; 'The most interesting person I have ever met'.

208 On target

messy

You will need :

> Blindfolds or scarves
> Spray foam
> A packet of Smarties or similar small sweets
> Plastic cups

Set a time limit for this game. Half the players, or a selected number, pick a partner. One of the pair lies blindfolded on the floor and a plastic cup is placed on their forehead. Their partner stands above them and, from waist height, tries to spray the foam into the cup, then drop six Smarties onto the foam. The winners are the pair with the most foam and Smarties in their cup.

209 Paper delivery

lots of space   team game

You will need:

> Sacks or strong blankets with 2 m of rope tied on two of the corners
> Newspapers
> Chairs
> A polished floor is an advantage for this game, which should not be played on a poor surface.

Lines of six chairs, spaced at 2m intervals, are positioned in the playing area. There should be one line for each team. Place piles of six newspapers for each team on the starting line. The players form teams of three, consisting of two 'horses' and one 'paper boy'. The paper boy sits on the sack and is dragged along the line of chairs by the horses. He tries to deliver one newspaper to each seat as they go. At the end of the course, the team returns to the starting point, where the next three players take over the task. At the end of the game, count the papers and award one point for every paper on the seats. Subtract a penalty point for each paper that has missed its target and landed on the floor.

This game has good spectator value.

210 Pass the Key

messy   team game

You will need:

> a long piece of string for each team
> one key and a dishcloth for each team
> a bucket of water for each team

Tie a key onto one end of the pieces of string and a dishcloth onto the other. Hide the buckets of water behind a screen and leave the end of each string with the dishcloth on it, in the water.

Get the players to line up, one behind the other, in teams. Give the end of the string with the key attached, to the player in the line who is nearest the buckets. They must thread the key down through their outer layer of clothing, out of the bottom of their trousers, and then pass it to the next player who threads it up his clothing and out the top before passing it on. This continues so that the key on the piece of string is threaded up and down alternate players' clothing and they are linked by the string. Eventually, the other end of the string, with the wet dishcloth attached, will be pulled into the first player's clothing. Wait for the screams!

211 Passing the Polo

team game

You will need:

Packets of Polo mints or similar confectionery with a hole in the centre
Enough toothpicks for all players.
This is not a game for small children.

Divide the players into equally numbered teams, and sit them in circles or lines. Each player holds a toothpick between her teeth. The Polo mint is passed down the line of players from toothpick to toothpick. Handling is strictly forbidden. The first team to pass the mint right round the circle, or completely down the line, is the winner. If the Polo is dropped by any member of a team, it must be passed back to the first player and begin its journey again.

212 Peg a person

lots of space

You will need:

A supply of durable clothes pegs

Give six clothes pegs to each player and set a time limit. The idea is to get rid of your pegs by pinning one on six different players, while you keep moving to avoid being pegged yourself. Even if you succeed in getting rid of all your pegs, you continue playing by avoiding the other peg hangers.

At the end of the time limit, the person with the least pegs on him is the winner.

213 Pinball soccer

lots of space   team game

You will need:

A football and newspapers

This game is best played indoors on a smooth surface.

Set up a goal at each end of the playing area and divide the players into two teams. Scatter the newspapers evenly, one for every team member, all over the playing area. Keeping one foot on their newspapers, players kick the ball towards their opponents' goal. Any player taking his foot off his newspaper goes in the 'sin bin' and is not allowed to take part for an agreed penalty time.

214 Romantic letters

team game

You will need:

Newspapers
Scissors
Glue
Sheets of plain paper

Teams of four to six players are each given a supply of the above items. The aim is for each team to compose a really soppy love letter within a time limit (eg 15 minutes). They must choose the words from the newspapers, cut them out and stick them in the most romantic order on the plain sheet of paper. These are later read out to all the groups. At the end take a clapometer poll to select the best composition. A suitable prize could be a large chocolate heart.

215 Shoe kicking

lots of space

No equipment needed

All players should be wearing shoes for this game. Competitors stand in a line, take off one shoe and dangle it from the end of their foot. They then take it in turns to see who can kick their shoe the furthest.

Supervision is needed as shoes can fly all over the place. Spectators need to stand well back!

216 Shoe shucking

team game

You will need:

A washing-up bowl filled with water for each team

Girls will need to wear trousers and shorts for this game. Divide into teams of six. Team members lie on their backs, with their feet in the air and touching in the centre of a circle. Place the container of water on their elevated feet. The team then works together to allow each team member to remove their shoes without spilling any water. The winning team is the one with the most shoes off after four minutes.

217 Sock it

You will need:

A length of cord or washing line
Twenty numbered old socks
Pegs
Twenty 'mystery' items
A paper and pencil for each player

Each sock, containing a mystery item is pegged securely on the washing-line. Competitors move down the line, feeling the item in each sock. They may use only one hand at a time, and they must feel all twenty or so items before any writing is allowed. Players then have five minutes to write down what they think the items in the socks are. The player who has guessed the most correctly when the time is up is the winner.

This may also be played as a team game – the team with the highest number of correct guesses is declared the winner. However, if played as a team game, comparing lists between team members is forbidden.

If you want a quiet game, why not suggest no talking throughout the competition.

218 Sock shop

more than 15

No equipment needed

This is a noisy but hilarious game, which needs to be played in a dark room. You will need a good number of players for it to be viable. Half the players remove their shoes and one sock, and throw them into a pile in the centre of the room. They then sit in a circle around the pile. their bare feet stretched out in front of them.

The lights are switched off and the other players immediately run from the edge of the circle to gather a sock and two shoes. In the dark, they try to find a bare foot, dress it with the sock and get the shoes onto the feet. If any shoe won't fit, it is returned to the pile in the middle and another shoe taken. After the time limit expires, lights go on. The successful player is the one who is most successful at matching the sock and the shoes with their rightful owner.

219 Team refreshments

messy team game

You will need:

Paper cups filled with water
One dry biscuit for each player

In teams, the players stand in a line, side by side, facing forwards. Their hands are tied together. On a signal, each team attempts to pass the biscuits down the line so that every player has one. When all the team have eaten the biscuits, the cups of water are passed down and every player must drink the cup dry. This is a great game for teaching reliance on each other.

220 Serious laughter

team game

No equipment needed

Divide the players into two or more teams. The first person in each team lies on the floor, the next does the same but with his head on the first person's stomach. All the others in the team follow suit.

When the teams are settled, the first person in each team has to shout 'Ha!' Number two follows 'Ha, Ha!'. Number three, 'Ha, Ha, Ha!', and so on. This is a serious business! No smiling or laughing is permitted, and any group breaking the rules has to start again. The team to complete the process three times without laughing is the winner.

221 The two hats

You will need:

Two hats

All the players stand in a row. One person is given two hats and is named the 'hat man'. He then walks along the row and presents one hat to any player he chooses. The moment someone receives the hat she must do everything contrary to that being done by the hat man, who keeps possession of the other hat. If he puts the hat on his head, his counterpart must keep hers off. If he holds it in his left hand, the other holds it in her right hand; if he sits down, the other must stand up, and so on. If the first player finds that no mistakes are being made he goes on to another and tries different tactics. Once the second player makes an error, she is out and returns to sit in line with the others.

222 Three back race

No equipment needed

Teams of six, nine or twelve players line up behind a starting line. The first three players link arms, with their backs facing inward, and race the other team to the finishing line and back. They then touch the next three, who do the same. The team to finish first is the winner.

223 Tightrope test

You will need:

White tape
A pair of binoculars

Stretch or stick a white tape across the floor. Each player attempts to walk along the tape, peering through the wrong end of the binoculars. It is surprisingly difficult. Give the laughing onlookers a chance to try it for themselves.

224 Tipping the waste

team game

You will need:

Plastic bin-bags filled with inflated balloons and tied securely

Divide the players into three teams. Two teams lie down, 3 m apart, in rows facing each other (see diagram). A third team makes a human wall standing between the teams lying down – they are the wall guardians.

Battle begins when the bin-bags are tossed to the teams lying down and they attempt to kick them over the human wall to score a point. The wall guardians obviously try to prevent this by intercepting the bags. When both teams are attempting to kick the bags over at the same time, confusion often occurs in the wall. The guardians may only use their hands and arms to block the bags.

Keep a tally of the points, then switch the teams after a given time so that everyone has the chance to be the human wall.

225 Title miming

You will need:

A list of well-known books, films, songs, hymns, carols or radio and television programmes

Each player chooses a title from the list, or is given one, and in turn, mimes it for the rest of the group to guess. They can either mime the whole title or divide their performance into 'scenes', each representing a word or syllable. The player who gets the maximum number of correct answers is the winner.

226 Toilet roll capers

team game

You will need:

A number of toilet rolls

Divide players into teams of ten or less. Each team lines up single file. The first player in a team is given a toilet roll. When the signal is given, he holds on to the end of the roll while the team unwinds the paper overhead until it reaches the last in line. He then lets go and the last player has to wind it back into a roll, then feed it back overhead to the front player who, in turn, rewinds it and holds the toilet roll above his head shouting, 'Rolled up, rolled up!'. The team to complete the process first is the winner.

227 Trussing

team game

You will need:

Handkerchiefs or suitable material for binding hands together
Two broomsticks

This may be played as a competitive team game. Two players sit on the floor. Each person's hands are bound together, palm to palm; their feet are also tied together at the ankles. Legs are drawn up under chins, heels rest on the floor, arms pass over the knees with the hands joined. The broomstick is passed over the arms and under the knees. The player resembles a chicken trussed on a skewer.

Competitors are placed toe to toe, opposite each other. One person attempts to turn her opponent on his back or side using of her toes. Award points for every successful throw. The team or player with the most points is the winner.

228 Tube stations

You will need:

Prepared papers and pencils for each participant

For those unfamiliar with the London Underground system, maps and charts are available from London Transport.

Players have to guess the names of the stations from the twenty-four clues within a given time. The person with the most correct answers is the winner.

Questions	Answers
1 Egg-shaped	*Oval*
2 Dark monks	*Blackfriars*
3 Home of Moriarty's enemy	*Baker Street*

4	Continental retreat	*Swiss Cottage*
5	Top people's open space	*Park Royal*
6	What a holy man sees	*Parsons Green*
7	Do rabbits live here?	*Warren Street*
8	Where do you lose your head?	*Tower Hill*
9	Coloured river crossing	*Redbridge*
10	The grieving widow	*Victoria*
11	Find it with wings and a halo	*Angel*
12	Place for spreading the good news	*Gospel Oak*
13	Sounds like a football team has captured the street	*Tottenham Court Road*
14	Won on the playing fields of Eton	*Waterloo*
15	Canine cries	*Barking*
16	John O'Gaunt's portal	*Lancaster Gate*
17	Shakespeare country	*Stratford*
18	Royal Road	*Queensway*
19	Leave your money here	*Bank*
20	1,760 yards gone	*Mile End*
21	Rough seas do this to some people	*Turnham Green*
22	This dyke needs supporting	*Shoreditch*
23	Burial place for soldiers	*Gunnersbury*
24	A farmhand's shrub	*Shepherd's Bush*

229 Twenty questions

team game

You will need:

A list of places, famous people or animals

Form two teams of three or four persons. Choose a word from the list and tell the teams what category the word belongs to. They each then have twenty questions in which to guess what it is. The leader can only answer 'Yes' or 'No' or 'Don't know'. The team who guesses correctly within twenty questions is awarded points. The game is played by alternate teams.

If teams are large enough, rotate different panels for each word so that everyone can participate.

230 Vacancy!

You will need:

A strong chair for each player

This is a very active game. Everyone sits on chairs arranged in a circle, facing inwards. One player leaves his chair and stands in the centre. He tries to quickly sit on a vacant seat while the rest of the group moves to the right, trying to block him. When he is finally successful the person on his immediate left has to take his place in the centre of the circle.

231 Wink and run

team game

You will need:

One chair for every other player

Arrange a circle of chairs in a circle, facing inwards. Divide players into two equally numbered groups. One group stands one behind each chair, and the other group sits on the chairs. Those seated 'make a contract' by winking at another seated person, then they quickly swap seats with each other. Meanwhile, the people standing behind the chairs try to prevent them from doing this. They stand with their hands by their sides until their partner on the chair tries to move, and then they quickly try to restrain them by grabbing their shoulders. They may not, however, move in front of the chair to stop them. If they are too slow, and their partner manages to swap seats, they find themselves with a new partner to keep in place. If the swapping pair are unable to change because one or other is restrained, they must stay where they are until they can try again.

Swap groups after a while, so that everyone has a turn.

232 Walk the line

You will need:

String or tape
Sellotape
Hand mirror

Take a 4 m long piece of string or tape and place it on the floor, stretched out. Sellotape each end to the floor. Each player holds a hand mirror above his head and tries to walk along the string by looking into the mirror. The winner is the one to reach the other end without stepping off the line.

233 What a character

You will need:

Ten to twenty faces (see examples) on card and numbered
Paper and pencils

Set a time limit for players to write in a few words, the last sentence they think each face might have just heard. Then they read them out to the group. The winner is the one to get the most applause.

Other variations could be to say why they would like to invite each character on a date, or what each of the characters might be thinking.

234 What a surprise!

You will need:

A number of small surprise gifts, well-wrapped but tangible, eg a tie, a sausage, a bottle (Ask people to bring a small parcel of something they would gladly throw out in a spring clean.)
A large card, attached to each parcel
Pencils

The players sit in a circle and pass the parcels around. When the music stops, each player feels the mystery parcel they are holding and then writes on the card how he thinks the recipient of such a gift could use it. The music starts up again, and the parcels go round the circle again. Each time the music stops, another comment is added by a different player.

When there are about six or seven comments on each card, one by one, each player with a parcel reads the comments on the card, then opens the parcel to reveal the surprise gift.

7 Games with balloons

235 Balloon bursting

team game

You will need:

A chair for each team
A balloon for each player
Masking tape, paint or chalk to mark the starting line

Mark out a starting line and place the chairs side by side about 5 m in front of it. Blow up the balloons and place one balloon on each chair. Equally numbered teams stand behind the starting line and, on a signal, the first player in each team runs to the chair in front of their team. They try to burst the balloon on the chair by sitting on it, and then race back to the start. The players race in turn, and the team to finish first is the winner.

A variation on this game is for each player to tie a balloon to his ankle, then tread on and burst the other players' balloons while trying to keep their own safe. The last player with his balloon intact wins. Warn players beforehand to take care that they don't kick each other by accident in the excitement.

236 Balloon crackers

You will need:

Balloons
Paper
Some small prizes

Write numbers on tiny slips of paper and insert them inside the balloons before they are inflated. The numbers should be matched by those on the prizes. When they are blown up, hang the balloons in such a manner that they can be released together.

During the party, tell the players that there are numbers in the balloons and that some are worth prizes. The balloons are then released. As the balloons float down from above, much fun results as players try to burst the balloons and retrieve the numbers.

237 Balloons in the bucket

team game

You will need:

Two blown up balloons
Two rolled-up newspapers
Two boxes

Two teams stand in lines parallel to each other. Place the boxes at the head of the teams, and give a balloon and a newspaper to the first person in each team. He has to take the balloon round the length of the team, keeping it in the air by hitting it with the rolled-up paper, and get it back into the box. However, he may only use one hand to do this. If he fails to keep the balloon aloft, and it drops to the ground, he must go back and start again. When he successfully completes his round, the next player takes over, and so on, until all the team have had a turn. The first team to finish wins.

238 Balloon on the rails

team game

You will need:

Balloons
String
Several curtain rings
Cream crackers

Stretch as many string lines as there are teams between chairs. On each line hang a balloon secured to a curtain ring. Competing teams line up single file and, in turn, players blow their balloons from one end of their team line to the other. The handicap, however, is that each competitor has to eat two cream crackers before blowing the balloon!

This may also be organised as a relay race, with the number of relay teams depending on the number of players.

239 Balloon shavers

messy

You will need:

Balloons
Razors
Cans of shaving foam
Music
Pins (optional)

You may wish to cover the playing area with a sheet or newspaper, in case of any mess. Divide the players into two teams. One team sits on chairs, facing the audience; each with a blown-up balloon in their teeth. The other team stand behind them, holding the cans of shaving cream. They cover the balloons with shaving cream and then on the word 'go' they attempt to shave the balloons while music is playing.

The game often ends with no balloons bursting, but the anticipation is always good and the audience will enjoy it. At the end you can secretly give the shavers a pin each, and on 'Go' they can burst the balloons.

240 Balloon shower

messy

You will need:

A balloon filled with water for each pair

This game is best played outdoors.

Pairs face each other in lines about a metre apart. One line holds the water-filled balloons. On the command 'Go' they throw the balloons to their partners who, hopefully, catch them. If a balloon bursts, the pair is out. On the next round, the pairs step back, making the gap between them wider. The process is repeated, widening the gap for each round, until all the balloons have burst.

241 Balloon smash

You will need:

> *Balloons*
> *String*
> *Masking tape*
> *Newspapers*

Give everyone a balloon and a piece of string each. The balloon is blown up and tied around the waist, so it hangs behind the player's back. Each player makes a 'balloon smasher' out of rolled-up newspaper and masking tape. The object is to pop other players' balloons by hitting them with your balloon smasher, while protecting your own balloon by moving around as quickly as possible. Once someone's balloon is popped, she is out of the game. The last to remain in the game wins.

242 Balloon tossing

You will need:

> *Ten or more balloons filled with water and securely tied (it is helpful to the scorer to have two different-coloured sets of balloons)*
> *Two strong blankets or canvases of a similar size*

Divide the players into two teams and give them an equal amount of balloon ammunition. Each team spreads itself around a blanket, holding it like a fireman's rescue canvas.

Team members attempt to shoot balloons, one at a time, from their blanket into the opposition's blanket. This is done by dipping and angling the blanket with the balloon in the centre, so that when the team pulls outward the balloon is propelled into the air (and hopefully into the other team's blanket!). The team with the most balloons on target is the winner.

It is a good idea to set a time limit and, in view of the water involved, the game is probably best played outside.

243 Bin-bag ball

You will need:

> *Plastic bin-bags*
> *Balloons*

Place the inflated balloons into the bin-bags and tie them securely. Teams lie flat on the floor, in lines, facing the ceiling. Each player's feet rest on the shoulder of the person directly in front. On a given signal, the players pass the bags overhead using only their hands and arms. When the bag reaches the last in line, she runs to the front, lies down and passes the bag back again. When all players have had a turn at being number one, the team jumps to their feet.

244 Hugging honey

You will need:

> *Three balloons for each pair of competitors*

Each pair is given three balloons. On a given signal, they inflate all three balloons, then one of the pair places a balloon under each armpit and sits on the third. Her partner tries to burst the balloons by hugging her and sitting on her knees. The first pair to succeed in bursting all three balloons is the winner.

This can be particularly fun at a Valentine's party.

245 Spacemen

lots of space *team game*

You will need:

Several referees
Plenty of balloons and string, enough for each player and lots of spares
Masking tape or chalk to mark the lines

Mark a line at each end of a playing area and agree a playing time in advance. The players form two equally numbered teams. A leader for each team is appointed, and he wears something distinctive so as not to be easily identified. Each player ties a balloon on their wrist – this is their 'life support system'. The aim of the game is to acquire the greatest number of team points. A point is awarded for every balloon burst. The balloons may only be burst by hand: no pins or other 'weapons' are allowed. When a life support system is broken, the player is dead and must lie on the ground. A dead comrade may be rescued and carried back to the home base-line by members of his team, where a new support system is attached to his wrist. The player is now alive again and may resume combat.

The team must do all they can to protect their leader by circling and blocking the opposing team. If a leader's life-support system is broken, then he is captured and taken behind the opposition's base-line. The team who captured him is awarded ten points. The leader cannot struggle, neither may his team rescue him.

The game ends when all of one team's life-support systems have been broken or at the end of the allotted time. Sometimes it is necessary to stop the game temporarily so that the referees can count the dead: the command for this should be 'Freeze'. To recommence, the command word is 'Combat'.

Players will appreciate playing several rounds so as to develop their techniques and skills.

8 Paper and pencil games

246 Antiques and bygones

team game

You will need:

A quantity of objects from the past, large or small, and preferably over fifty years old

Hide the objects from view, then show them, one by one, to the players. Divide the players into two or four groups. The first team to call the correct name of the item is awarded points. Further points may be given for other specific information, eg near date of manufacture, original place of invention, country of origin.

This game is educational as well as fun and often tests the imaginative skills of the participants.

247 Aunt Agatha's agony column

You will need:

Pencil and paper for each player

Give everyone a small piece of paper and a pencil, and ask them to write, at the top of the paper, a problem or dilemma in one sentence, eg 'If I had my toe stuck in a lift door...' 'If my nose got caught in a sausage machine...' 'If my wig fell off...'. They then fold the papers down over the sentence and pass them to someone else. That person must write a solution without looking at the problem. When they have finished, choose the best of the hilarious results and read them out.

248 Autograph collecting

You will need:

A prepared list of characteristics for each player (see below)
Pencils

The statements given below may be adapted to suit local people and circumstances, and the number taking part.

Armed with the list and a pencil, players move around, asking questions with a view to collecting signatures next to the characteristics that apply to those signing. They may only approach one person at a time, and that person must be truthful in their response. A collector cannot have the same signature more than once on their list. To ensure that people get to know each other, say that they must introduce themselves by name before they can get a signature. The first person to collect all the signatures, or to collect the most, is the winner.

Uses Colgate toothpaste	Talks to themselves	Is wearing earrings	Can whistle God save the Queen
Likes mustard	Has long hair	Plays chess regularly	Has slept in a tent
Loves Bach	Uses after-shave	Has driven a motor cycle	Has a hole in their sock
Has eaten a snail	Is ticklish	Has grey hair	Has never ridden a horse
Can touch their nose with their tongue	Has a sweet tooth	Listens to Radio 1	Sings in the bath
Watches Neighbours	Walks under ladders	Has a Barclaycard	Likes detective stories
Likes Stilton cheese	Still has tonsils	Has broken their arm or leg	Squeezes toothpaste in the middle
Watches Coronation Street	Did not make their bed today	Can do the splits	Is a food fanatic
Writes poetry	Is wearing grey socks	Owns a dog	Saves stamps

249 Baby show

You will need:

Pencil and paper for each player
Two small prizes

Beforehand, invite those taking part to bring the earliest photo of themselves that they possess. Ask them to write their names on the back. Fix the photos to sheets of paper, give each a number and display them around the room.

Provide everyone with a numbered paper and a pencil. They then go round the room, inspecting the pictures and guessing the names of the babies. The guesses are recorded against the appropriate number on their paper. The next stage is for them to choose the prettiest baby, recording on their paper the number they have chosen. Give a prize to the player who guessed the greatest number of names correctly and award five bonus points to those who chose the most popular prettiest baby. The person with the highest aggregate score is the overall winner, deserving of the other prize.

250 Bishop's riddle

You will need:

Small cards, each with a riddle and numbered (see the list below)
Paper and pencil for each player

This game is attributed to an Oxford bishop, possibly Bishop Wilberforce.

Tell the players that the answers to these riddles are all parts of the body. Put the riddles up around the room and set a time limit to solve the riddles. Answers are in italics.

1	I have a trunk	*The body*
2	It has two lids	*Eyelids*
3	It has two caps	*Kneecaps*
4	Two musical instruments	*Eardrums*
5	I kick with two measurements	*Feet*
6	Carpenters can't do without them	*Nails*
7	I stand on two good fish	*Soles*
8	Lots of small shellfish	*Muscles (mussels)*
9	Trees in my hands	*Palms*
10	Flowers to kiss with	*Two lips (tulips)*
11	Two young animals	*Calves*
12	Lots of small wild animals	*Hares (hares)*
13	A fine stag	*Heart (hart)*

14	Whips without handles	*Lashes*
15	Weapons of war	*Arms*
16	Lots of weathercocks	*Veins (vanes)*
17	A regiment marches like this	*Instep*
18	The two sides you can take when voting in Parliament	*Eyes and nose (ayes and noes)*
19	Two students provide a good view	*Pupils*
20	A number of senior Cambridge university members	*Tendons (ten dons)*
21	A big wooden box	*Chest*
22	Two fine religious buildings	*Temples*
23	The product of camphor trees	*Gums*
24	A piece of old English money	*Crown*
25	Artists use this	*Palate (palette)*
26	Rowers use this	*Skull (scull)*
27	It crosses a river	*Bridge (of nose)*
28	They have blades you can't cut with	*Shoulders*
29	The twelfth letter of the alphabet finished with a bow	*Elbow (L+bow)*
30	Instruments used in church music	*Organs*

11	Flowers to see through	*Irises*
12	Animals in burrows	*Hairs (hares)*
13	Hills have these	*Brow*
14	Flowers to kiss with	*Two lips (Tulips)*
15	A plumber often deals with these	*Joints*
16	Employees	*Hands*
17	It crosses rivers	*Bridge*
18	Measurement before metric	*Foot*
19	Military bands would be lost without this instrument	*Drum*
20	A place of worship found in the Old Testament	*Temple*
21	Hedgerow berries	*Hips*
22	Extravagance	*Waist (waste)*
23	An old word for containers	*Vessels (blood)*
24	Long-distance luggage	*Trunk*

251 Body language

You will need:

Small cards, each with a clue and numbered (see the list below)
Pencils and paper

Display the clues around your meeting-place. Give each participant paper and a pencil on which to write their answers. Set a time limit for the participants to try and find the solutions: they are all parts of the body.

1	A kind of shellfish	*Muscles (Mussels)*
2	A salt-water fish	*Sole*
3	A part of marble stone	*Veins*
4	Young animals bred on farms	*Calves*
5	Scholars at school	*Pupils*
6	Another name for a box cover	*Lid*
7	Combs have these	*Teeth*
8	Trees in a desert	*Palms*
9	A table needs these for support	*Legs*
10	Lots of personal pronouns	*Eyes*

252 Book game

You will need:

Large cards
A marker pen
Pencils and paper

Write the names of the books and their authors on separate cards, with the titles numbered. Place these cards around your meeting place. Hand out the paper and pencils and ask the players to match the book title with the author's name. The first person to match them all is the winner.

A variation on this game would be to hand out a list of titles of books (these may be real or fictional) and, in groups of three or four, players make up names for the authors. Here are some examples:

Book title	*Author*
English Summer	Howitt Raynes (How it rains)
Let us Pray	Neil Down (Kneel down)
The Godfather	M. Afia

Read out their offerings at the end of the allotted time. The group getting the greatest laughter or applause is the winner.

253 Book reviews

more than 15

You will need:

Paper and pencil for each player

This game is played along the pattern of Consequences, with the leader giving the players directions as the game proceeds. It is suitable for ten or more players.

The players begin by writing at the top of their pieces of paper a real or imaginary book title. They then fold the paper over, so that what they have written cannot be seen, and pass it to the person on their right. When everyone has done this, they must think of, or invent, the name of a subtitle. They write this as near to the top of their papers as possible, under the first fold. The papers are folded, to hide the subtitle, and the papers continue to rotate until some or all of the following have been added to them:

The name of the author (real or imaginary)
A brief extract from the book (limit the number of words or lines)
Another brief extract from the book
A paper in which a review of the book appeared
What the review said
Another paper in which a review appeared
What the review said
The name of the person who bought the first copy
What he or she did with it

When all the items have been written down, the papers then pass on one or more places. Then each player unfolds the paper in his possession and reads what is in front of him. Alternatively, the leader can read out all the contributions.

254 Bosses and secretaries

You will need:

Newspaper cuttings (all of equal length)
Pencils and paper

You will need four to eight players on each team. Half the team are the bosses, the others are their secretaries. Give the newspaper cuttings to the bosses, and a pencil and paper to each secretary. The bosses stand about 4m away from their secretaries, facing them (if space allows). All speaking at the same time, each boss then dictates the contents of the newspaper cutting to their secretary who takes it down. The first pair with a complete record of a reasonably accurate dictation are the winners.

You might like to complicate the game by putting large sweets in the bosses' mouths before they start to dictate.

255 Beetle

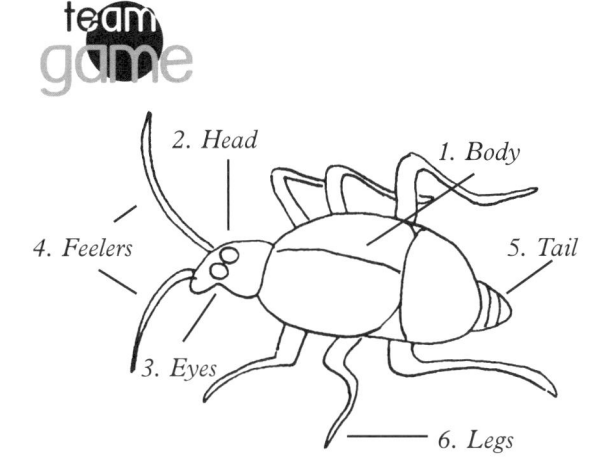

team game

2. Head   1. Body
4. Feelers   5. Tail
3. Eyes
6. Legs

You will need:

A copy of the beetle diagram for each team
Pencils, a dice and a cup for each team

Divide players into teams of four. Have a player from one team sit in while another plays, to check for fairness. Decide beforehand the number of rounds you are going to play.

Team members throw the dice in turn. The object is to put an X on each part of the beetle's body when the corresponding number comes up on the dice. Every part of the body must be 'X-ed' individually, eg the group will need to throw '6' six times to 'X' each leg. Obviously, the quicker the team can pass the dice for another throw, the better chance they have of winning.

When every part of the beetle is 'X-ed', the team yells, 'Beetle!'. The teams total their scores, which are noted, and another round begins.

256 Car names

You will need:

Small cards, each with a clue and numbered (see the list below)
Paper and a pencil for each player

This is definitely a game for the car enthusiast, as each sentence suggests a car name. Place the clues around the venue (or give a prepared clue sheet to each player). Set a time limit for players to go round the clues and write their answers. The winner is the person with the highest number of correct answers.

Another way to play could be to have separate clue and answer cards which players can match.

1. A jungle animal — *Jaguar*
2. Paris underground — *Metro*
3. The mint with a hole in it — *Polo*
4. A flower — *Lotus*
5. Cowboy greeting — *Audi (Howdy!)*
6. Good name for a dog — *Rover*
7. One on whom you can depend — *Reliant*
8. You could drive this around an eighteen-hole course — *Golf*
9. Made to make your mouth water — *Opel (fruit)*
10. A companion for a social occasion — *Escort*

257 Christmas introduction

You will need:

An instruction sheet for each player (see below)
Pencils

This is a good starter for a Christmas occasion and may be adapted to suit local circumstances. Give everyone a paper and pencil, and tell them they must fulfil all the instructions on the sheet and collect other people's initials as they go

1. Get five autographs (first, middle and last names).

2. Find three other people and sing together, 'We wish you a merry Christmas', as loudly as you can. Then get them to initial your paper here:
   ....

3. Tell someone the names of three of Santa's reindeers.
   Initials ....

4. Pretend you are Santa Claus. Find someone of the opposite sex, sit him or her on your lap and ask what he or she wants for Christmas.
   Initials ....

5. Tell someone what three gifts the wise men brought Jesus.
   Initials ....

6. Pick the ornament on the Christmas tree which you like best (or some other Christmas feature at the venue). Find someone else and give them a fifteen-second speech on why you like that particular ornament.
   Initials ....

7. You are Ebenezer Scrooge. Find someone and ask them to wish you a Merry Christmas. When they do, say 'Bah! Humbug!' ten times while jumping up and down.
   Initials ....

8. Shake hands with someone wearing red or green.
   Initials ....

9. Tell someone who it was that tried to find out where Jesus was born in order to kill him.
   Initials ....

10. Shake hands and say 'It's really good to see you' to ten different people who belong to the following categories (you can make your own; collect one signature for each):

(a) Someone over 60 ....
(b) Someone under 14 ....
(c) Someone who's a good cook ....
(d) Someone who you think would look good in a kilt ....
(e) Someone taller than you ....
(f) Someone wearing earrings ....
(g) Someone who's got grey hair ....
(h) The person in the room who's been married the longest ....
(i) Someone who had cornflakes for breakfast this morning ....
(j) Someone who knows what they're getting for Christmas ....

258 Americanisms

You will need:

Cards, each with a word/phrase as listed below
Pencils and paper

Place the cards around the room. Set a time limit as the players try to match the American equivalent with the English term. The player who gets the most correct is the winner.

USA	English
Billfold	Wallet
Bobby pin	Hairgrip
Diaper	Nappy
Drapes	Curtains
Druggist	Chemist/ pharmacist
Faucet	Tap
Fender	Bumper (of a car)
Hood	Bonnet (of a car)
Intern	Junior hospital doctor/ houseman
Kerosene	Paraffin+
Mortician	Undertaker/funeral director
Muffler	Car silencer
Odometer	Mileometer
Pacifier	Baby's dummy
Podiatrist	Chiropodist
Realtor	Estate agent
Rummage sale	Jumble sale
Rutabaga	Swede, root vegetable
Skillet	Frying pan
Sophomore	Second-year student
Suspenders	Braces
Thumbtack	Drawing pin
Tick-tack-toe	Noughts and crosses
Truck farm	Market garden
Trunk	Boot of a car
Vest	Waistcoat
Veteran	Ex-serviceman
Zip code	Postcode

259 Country quiz

You will need:

A list of the following objects, numbered
A pencil for each player

The aim is to match the name of the object with the associated country of origin.

Have the answers unnumbered and jumbled in a second column on the same sheet, or put them on cards displayed around the walls of the venue. The list can be expanded ad lib.

Objects	Answers
1 Cricket	England
2 Eiffel Tower	France
3 Great Wall	China
4 Shamrock	Ireland
5 Sombrero	Mexico
6 Baseball	USA
7 Olympics	Greece
8 Pantheon	Italy
9 Diamonds	South Africa
10 Kimono	Japan
11 Yodelling	Switzerland
12 Pyramids	Egypt
13 Coffee	Brazil
14 Thistle	Scotland
15 Leek	Wales
16 Taj Mahal	India
17 Amazon	Brazil/Peru
18 Cossack	Russia
19 Pineapples	Hawaii
20 Sherpa	Nepal
21 Sugar	Cuba
22 Windmills	Holland

260 Drawing clumps

team game

You will need:

Paper and pencils
A list of drawable objects or events, eg monkey in a zoo, preacher in a pulpit, a coronation, a cow being milked
A small prize (optional)

Divide the players into teams. In turn, a member from each team comes up and is quietly given a different subject from the list. He returns to his group and has to draw the subject for the rest of his team to guess, without incorporating words that will give the game away. Whoever guesses the subject goes up for the next item on the list, until it is exhausted. The team exhausting the list first is the winner. You might like to award a prize for the funniest, simplest or best drawing.

261 Inventions

You will need:

A quiz sheet and a pencil for each player

Set a time limit for players to complete their quiz sheets.

1 What year were matches invented
(a)   1725
(b)   1827
(c)   1901

2 In which period was the idea for the modern computer first proposed
(a)   1802-1815
(b)   1860-1900
(c)   1914-1918

3 What year were four-wheel roller skates patented and where?
(a)   Chicago 1902
(b)   Liverpool 1830
(c)   Fulham London 1841
(d)   New York 1863

4 The safety razor was invented in 1901 by King Camp Gillette. How many razor blades had he sold by 1906?
(a)   9,000
(b)   1 million
(c)   12 million

5 When was the safety pin invented?
(a)   1684
(b)   1849
(c)   1902

6 Percy Shaw, a building contractor, invented cat's-eyes for roads in 1934. Was Shaw a native of...?
(a)   Minneapolis
(b)   Aberdeenshire
(c)   Herefordshire
(d)   Yorkshire

7 Jigsaw puzzles were first created as an educational aid by cartographer John Spilsbury. What year were they marketed?
(a)   1763
(b)   1842
(c)   1910

8 In what city was the first hair perm developed?
(a)   London
(b)   York
(c)   Chicago
(d)   Paris

9 Albert Parkhouse, of Michigan USA, first thought of the idea of a wire hanger in 1903. How much did he get for his patent?
(a)   10 million dollars
(b)   50,000 dollars
(c)   56 dollars
(d)   Nothing at all

10 When did William Rontgen discover the X-ray?
(a)   1895
(b)   1840
(c)   1903
(d)   1911

11 When did Clarence Birdseye invent his first fast-freezing machines?
(a)   1912
(b)   1843
(c)   1924

12 When did Dr Gorlitz, the director of a Polish sanatorium, first think of using dogs as guides for the blind?
(a)   1905
(b)   1916
(c)   1918

Answers
1 (b) by English chemist John Walker of Stockton on Tees.
2 (b) by the Victorian, Charles Babbage.
3 (d).
4 (c).
5 (b) by Walter Hunt of New York, USA.
6 (d).
7 (a).
8 (d).
9 (d) his boss got the cash!
10 (a).
11 (c) in the USA.
12 (b).

262 Jumbled names

You will need:

*Cards with jumbled names of places and people
Pencils and paper*

Place the cards around the room, and give the players paper and pencils. The cards should be printed clearly and numbered, eg LENGRLEF, IMAJACA, MIAL (answers: GRENFELL, JAMAICA, LIMA. Locate the places afterwards on a map, particularly if the game is being used as an introduction for study of a country.

263 Kim's game

You will need:

Paper and pencil for each player
A variety of objects
A tray

There are many variations of this game:

Option 1: Players sit in a circle, and a tray containing twenty or more objects is passed round, with each player noting the contents. The tray is then removed, paper and pencils are distributed, and the objects on the tray are listed from memory.

Option 2: A number of bottles or jars filled with scented objects are passed round the circle of players, who list the contents as they smell them. (Examples of smells could include a well known perfume, tomato ketchup, garlic or even a fresh herring!)

Option 3: A number of objects are placed in opaque bags and passed round the circle for people to identify by feeling the bag. Alternatively this can be played in the dark, in which case the players memorise the feel or smell of the objects and then list them later when the lights go on. (Have some articles which are similar in shape, such as a coin or a button, to complicate the game.)

264 Numbers game

You will need:

Clue sheets (see below)
Pencils

Players have to fill in the missing numbers on the clue sheets. The person with the most correct is the winner.

Alternatively, this may be played as a team game with the leader calling the statement and teams shouting back the answer. The first group to call the correct answer is awarded points. For calling a wrong answer a penalty point is deducted.

Clues
1. Ali Baba and the .... thieves
2. The .... Commandments
3. .... poster bed
4. .... ages of man (Shakespeare)
5. .... wise men
6. .... varieties (Heinz)
7. .... apostles
8. .... Island Dressing
9. .... horsemen of the Apocalypse
10. .... is company, ... 's a crowd
11. Into the valley of death, rode the ....
12. A tale of .... cities
13. There are .... players in a football team
14. Judas and the .... pieces of silver
15. .... cheers
16. .... bears
17. .... pins
18. .... days has September
19. .... in hand
20. The .... Gospels
21. .... tribes of Israel
22. A bird in the hand is worth .... in the bush
23. The .... Musketeers

Answers
(1) 40; (2) 10; (3) 4; (4) 7; (5) 3; (6) 57; (7) 12; (8) 1,000; (9) 4; (10) 2 and 3; (11) 600; (12) 2; (13) 11 (14) 30; (15) 3; (16) 3; (17) 2; (18) 30; (19) 4; (20) 4; (21) 12; (22) 2; (23) 3.

265 Phobias

You will need:

Cards, each with a phobia clearly printed on it (see list below)
Pencils and papers

Place the cards around the room, where they are clearly visible. Set a time limit for players to write down the phobia and the excessive fear it describes. The person with the most correct at the end is the winner.

Phobia	*Fear of*
Aerophobia	Drafts
Zoophobia	Animals
Ornithophobia	Birds
Haemophobia	Blood
Claustrophobia	Confined spaces
Scotophobia	The dark
Necrophobia	Death or dead bodies
Potophobia	Drink
Spermophobia	Germs
Phasmophobia	Ghosts
Maniaphobia	Insanity
Nyctophobia	Night
Helminthophobia	Worms
Agoraphobia	Open spaces or going out
Pogonophobia	Beards
Lalophobia	Speaking or public speaking
Hydrophobia	Water or wetness

Gynephobia	Women or girls
Thermophobia	Heat
Acrophobia	Heights
Traumatophobia	Injury

266 Portraits

You will need:

A 'faces' sheet (see below)
Pencils

To prepare the 'faces' sheet, draw 10–15 small ovals (faces) on A4 size paper and fill in the eyes and noses. Photocopy one sheet for each person and provide them all with pencils.

Inform the group that they are all budding portrait painters. They must add features (eg mouth, hair, ears) to each face and see how many different faces each artist can create within a given time. The most original portrait artist is the winner.

267 Signatures

You will need:

A list of characteristics and pencils for each player (see below)

Another good ice-breaker. Give each person a list as they arrive. They then move around the room collecting signatures from those for whom the statements are true. They may only collect one signature at a time, and they cannot have the same signature more than once. When the time is up, the person with the most signatures is the winner.

Here is a sample questionnaire, but make up your own to fit local circumstances:

I can ski (on snow or water).....................
I commute to town each day ....
I'm wearing three rings ....
I wear size 5 shoes ....
I play an instrument ....
I'm an early riser ....
I find it difficult to get up in the morning
....
I prefer my own company to being in a crowd
....
I make my own clothes ....
I cook well ....
I don't like strawberries ....
I talk a lot ....
I have flown in an aircraft this year ....
I can speak more than two languages
....
I'm left-handed ....
I only read non-fiction books ....
I have met a famous TV/film personality
....

268 Sign up

You will need:

Papers and pencils

This game is a good mixer, enabling people to get aquainted.

Beforehand, write the word or words associated with your particular party or function down the left-hand side of an A4 sheet of paper (see below). Shorten or lengthen the word to match the size of your gathering and it may be helpful to know guests' names before you decide on the words. Give pencils and a copy of your word sheet to each player. They must try to get the others to sign the sheet: however, the condition is that the first letter in either their Christian or surname must correspond with one of the letters on the left-hand side of the paper. A player may sign another's paper only once.

Set a time limit. The person to collect the most signatures is the winner.

B	M	G	W	G	H
I	E	R	E	O	A
R	R	E	L	O	P
T	R	E	C	D	P
H	Y	T	O		Y
D		I	M	E	
A	C	N	E	V	A
Y	H	G		E	N
	R	S		N	N
G	I			I	I
R	S	F		N	V
E	T	R		G	E
E	M	I			R
T	A	E			S
I	S	N			A
N		D			R
G		S			Y
S					

269 Silent Christmas menu

You will need:

A mixed up menu for each player
Pencils

Without consulting each other, players, have to rearrange the letters to make items you would expect to find on a Christmas menu. Set a time limit. The person to get the most correct is the winner.

1	POTATO MOUS	Tomato soup
2	D MUD PULP GIN	Plum pudding
3	DARTSUC	Custard
4	SPINE MICE	Mince pies
5	FINF GUTS	Stuffing
6	A STEP TOO	Potatoes
7	CARBEDAUSE	Bread sauce
8	TOPSURS	Sprouts
9	EFFCOE	Coffee
10	EEL CRY	Celery
11	STAR OUKTERY	Turkey roast
12	SUNT	Nuts

270 Smells galore

You will need:

Small bags of herbs, flowers or vegetables with a distinct aroma
A list of the above for each player
Pencils

Make and number the bags beforehand. The players have to identify the bags' contents by their smell and write the number of the bag next to the item on the list. Set a time limit. The player to get the most right is the winner.

As a variation, have cheeses (eg Stilton, Cheshire, Danish Blue) or perfumes.

271 Tree game

You will need:

Ten identical tree-shaped cards with jumbled names and numbers (see example opposite).
Pencils and paper

Photocopy enough sets of trees and leaves for each player. Set a time limit for players to sort out the jumbled tree names and match the tree with the leaf belonging to it. The first to finish, or to get the most right by the end of the allotted time, is the winner.

Tree	Leaf
Horse Chestnut	f
Sycamore	h
Maple	b
Poplar	a
Willow	i
Beech	j
Ash	d
Hazel	g
Holly	e
Oak	c

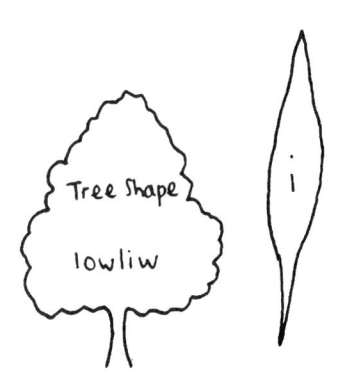

Example of a tree shape with it's corresponding leaf i. You will need to enlarge the illustrations when making up the cards.

ULTIMATE Games

9 Party fun and entertainment

Sometimes, introducing forfeits can make the games even more fun. You might like to use the following examples, or make up some of your own:
- Keep yawning until you can make somebody else yawn.
- Say the alphabet backwards.
- Stand on a chair and make a speech for two minutes on a given subject.
- Stand in the middle of the room in the varying positions described to you by six people.
- Blow a pea or bean over a given distance on the floor, with a straw.
- Lap up milk from a saucer.
- Laugh and cry ten times alternately.
- Sit on an balloon and burst it.
- Gargle with lemonade.
- Sing a song.

272 A human organ

You will need:

Eight single bedsheets
Nine players

Appoint one player to be the organist, and seat the other eight people in a row on a stage. Cover them with sheets, but leave their feet exposed. The organist assigns a different note of the scale to each person. She moves along the row, touching their feet. As she does so, they each raise that foot and sing their note. A person sings his note when his foot is raised and stops singing when his foot is lowered. The 'organist' can lift two different player's legs at a time, for more harmony!

273 Apple bobbing

You will need:

Apples
Onions
Blindfolds
A baby bath or child's paddling pool

Fill the tub with water. Contestants are blindfolded and kneel with their hands behind their back. On the command 'Go', they try to remove an apple from the tub. They then attempt to repeat the exercise with blindfolds on. After they have been blindfolded, however, the apples are removed and onions substituted. Encouraged by the spectators, players can often splash around for a considerable time before they discover the hoax.

274 Backside word shuffle

team game

You will need:

A set of cards, approximately 5cm square, for each team with a selected letter of the alphabet on each card (forget Q and Z)
A safety pin for each player

Attach the letters to the front of each player with the safety pins. In teams, the players have to spell words called out by the leader, using their letters. The words will be determined by the numbers playing and the letters available. The first team to spell a word correctly is the winner of that round.

275 Beautiful Betsie Brown

more than 15

You will need:

A narrator who can read the story imaginatively.

This is good entertainment for gatherings of 25+.

Assign a character to every member of the group (see the list below) and tell them what sound they should make when their particular character is mentioned during the narrative. This can be more fun if those making the sound have to stand to their feet when they are mentioned. However, when the storyteller says, 'Ride 'em cowboy', the entire group jump to their feet and scream their noises together.

Character noises:
Shadrach – Boo oo oo Boo oo
Betsie – Loud scream
Rattlesnakes – Hiss hiss, rattle rattle, hiss rattle
Cowboys – Yippee yippee
Love – Ahhhhh, cooooo
Bandits – Grrrr
Horses – Stamp feet
Guns – Bang bang
Wolves – Howling
Villains – Booooo
Cattle – Moo, Moo, Moo

Story

Way over the range, there lived a dashing, handsome, swashbuckling cowboy ..... named Jake Jones. His days were spent a'ridin' prairies on his piebald horse ..... called Noddy. His great passion in life was following the herds of bull-nosed bellowing cattle ..... That is, till he spied Betsie ..... Brown, a ravishing, young brunette riding a splendid horse ..... Jake's heart went 'Boom-didi-boom'.

Betsie ..... lived over the hill, with her doting parents, on a ranch where the cattle ..... were docile, and the cowboys ..... dull, and the rattlesnakes ..... roamed.

Now, Jake, the handsome cowboy ..... fell in love at first sight with Betsie ..... dashing over the range on her magnificent horse ..... named Upsey Daisie. He followed her on his horse ..... took one look into her subterranean deep blue eyes and fell off his horse ..... hopelessly in love .....

The cattle ..... the rattlesnakes ..... and even the wolves ..... were delighted.

Little did they know that the bold, bandy bandit ..... sharp-shooter, Shadrach ..... was a'spying on them. He quickly felt for his guns ..... and rode off to find his brother bandits ..... Now these bandits ..... were ugly. These bandits ..... were bad, and sharp-shooter Shadrach ..... the leader of the bandits ..... was a villain .....! Yep, I mean a villain .....! Yep, my friends a real villain ..... He was also in love ..... with Betsie ..... but the cowboys ..... using their guns ..... had always protected Betsie ..... from the amorous gun ..... loving villain ..... . He hated to hear the cowboys ..... shout, 'Ride 'em cowboy' ..... The bandits ..... planned an ambush. Sharp-shooter Shadrach ..... rode his horse ..... and the bandits ..... followed on their horses ..... . They saw Mr and Mrs Brown leave the ranch for the superstore.

The cows ..... looked up, the rattlesnakes ..... ran and the wolves ..... howled as the bandits ..... surrounded the ranch where Betsie ..... lived. They fired their guns .....

'At last I've got you, Betsie'..... said the bandit ..... Shadrach ..... .

Betsie left the rattlesnake ..... stew she was making and ran out of the house. She thought the cowboys ..... were firing their guns ..... When she saw the bandits ..... their guns ..... and the villains ..... Betsie cried out, 'Sharp-shooter Shadrach!'.....

He grabbed Betsie ..... pulled her onto his horse ..... and said 'Beautiful, beaming Betsie ..... you shall be my adoring wife. One day we will take over this ranch.'

Betsie ..... slapped his face. 'You villain ..... ' she cried. 'You villain ..... , you gun-loving bandit ..... villain ..... . I'll never be your wife, Shadrach ..... I don't love ..... you.'

'I'll throw you to the wolves' ..... cried the infuriated Shadrach, ... 'and my bandits ..... will kill your parents and feed them to the rattlesnakes .....' They fired their guns .....

Just then, the handsome cowboy ..... Jake came over the hill with his cowboys ..... . He saw the villain ..... and the bandits ..... and cried, 'Ride 'em cowboys!' Guns ..... fired, Betsie ..... was thrown to the ground. The cowboys ..... chased Sharp-shooter Shadrach ..... firing their guns ..... His sombrero was peppered with gun ..... bullets. His horses ..... pranced in anger. Betsie ..... cried. The bandits ..... fled to the hills where the wolves ..... all day, the cattle ..... and the rattlesnakes ..... The cowboys ..... crying 'Ride 'em cowboys!' ..... were still firing their guns ..... at the bandits ..... as they went over the hill with the cowboys ..... still in hot pursuit.

Betsie ..... looked up and saw the handsome cowboy..... He lifted her up. 'My love ..... my love ....., let us be wed, my love ..... . Let the wolves ....., let the bandits ....., let the cattle ..... be content, let the rattlesnakes ...., let the villains ..... never come again, let the guns ..... be silent.'

So they rode off into the sunset together forever, shouting 'Ride 'em cowboy' ..... .

The story could be even greater fun when local names are introduced. Why not try writing your own scripts?

276 Body charade

team game

No equipment needed

Divide the participants into two appropriately named groups. Four persons from each group are selected to act, and the rest have to guess what words they are spelling as they form the letters with their bodies (eg two actors, standing back to back, with arms outstretched in front of them form a 'T'). No fingers may be used to form individual letters. Each group must complete a word or phrase before the leader whispers the next word to the group's actors.

Examples of phrases that could be used, include: Two for tea, Blow your nose, How are you?, Nice day, Keep quiet, No entry, What's the time?, Goodnight.

277 Crazy walks

team game

No equipment needed

Divide players into teams of six or seven. Each player has to race over a given distance in a different manner. Here are some possibilities, but you could make up your own:
1 With every step taken, stop and yell 'Hooray' three times.
2 Dance like an elephant.
3 Hold your toe with one hand and your nose with the other.
4 Hop like a kangaroo.
5 Do roly-polys down the course (only if surface is clean and suitable).
6 Crawl on all fours.
7 Walk backwards shouting 'Look at me, look at me!'
8 Bend over so that your bottom is facing the finishing line, hold your ankles with your hands and walk to the line.

278 Dimensions

You will need:

Items readily found around your venue, eg windows, books, cake

Number each item. Players compete to guess their measurements or weight. Use scales and rulers to give accurate answers.

279 Celebration census

You will need:

*A sheet of instructions for each player (see below)
Pencils*

This is a game for a birthday party or similar celebration.

The players compete to fill in their sheets and collect signatures. They can only approach one peson at a time, and they cannot have the same signature more than once.

1 Get five autographs on the back of this sheet (including first, middle and last names and including their age).
2 Find someone of the opposite sex and play 'Pat a cake'. When finished, have your partner initial here .....
3 Have someone listen to you say, 'There's a chip shop in space that sells spaceship-shaped chips' ten times and then initial here .....
4 Have someone listen to you say correctly, 'The sixth sheikh's sheep is sick' six times, then initial here .....
5 Find someone who likes Jazz or Reggae music, then have them initial here .....
6 Have two people who have used toothpaste today, sign here:
   ....

7 Find someone whose age is within five years of yours. Initial .....
8 Find four people who are happy to be here. Get them to stand and shout, 'Wow! What a great party' (or something similar).
Initial: ....

280 Fashion parade

You will need:

*Clothes, hats, shoes, jewellery
Pencils and paper*

A player is sent out of the room to dress in as many garments, jewellery, hats, etc, as she can wear. The others are told that a model will be parading some new fashions. The model strolls in and models the clothes in the centre of the room for one minute. She goes out again, and the others try to list the items she was wearing, which she was not wearing when she first went out. Award one point for each correct item, and deduct two points for an incorrect one.

281 Foot word shuffle

You will need:

A felt marker, or poster paint and brush

This is a variation on 'Backside word shuffle' but here players have a letter painted on or stuck to the soles of their feet. You will need to make sure that the floor is clean before playing this game.

The teams lie on their backs in a row, with feet facing the audience. When a word is called, without getting up the players have to move over each other to spell the word with their feet. The resulting contortions and mixed up limbs will make this hilarious fun for the audience.

It is useful to have a non-lettered captain for each team who can 'bully' the teams into order and avoid too many spelling mistakes.

282 Guess a weight!

You will need:

To have weighed the four parading players privately, before the game commences

Three or four players are 'paraded' around the room while the rest of the party observes and guesses their combined weight. Then with much ceremony, some bathroom scales are unwrapped and each selected player is weighed. The person guessing the correct weight is the winner.

Guessing could also be done in teams.

283 Invisible make-up

You will need:

> Two small plates, one with soot or mascara on the underside

Explain that you have invented a new make-up which is invisible until exposed to daylight. At great expense (of course), you have come to demonstrate this wonderful new cosmetic. A volunteer is then seated opposite. He is given strict instructions to keep looking straight into your eyes, and he must do exactly what you do.

Give him the sooty plate doing the following routine with the unsooty one.

First, rub your index finger on top of the plate, then between your eyes and on your forehead. Then rub the plate's rim and apply to the side of your face. Finally, rub your finger three times firmly on the bottom of the plate, and then apply on your nose. The volunteer is completely unaware of the sooty image being created, which makes the audience laugh. At the end, give him a mirror to see the result.

284 Last chance

No equipment needed

Four volunteers are invited to share a raft in the mid-Atlantic. As their plight becomes more desperate, it is quite obvious that the raft can only support one person adequately and supplies will run out. Each of the four must give a speech in which he seeks to persuade the others that he has the greatest contribution to make to society and should therefore be the one to stay on the raft. This game could have a semi-serious slant, say, if you suggest four professions, eg a doctor, a minister of religion, a great conductor or musician, a millionaire philanthropist. Alternatively, introduce a humorous twist, with characters such as Father Christmas, Snow White, Donald Duck or Yogi Bear.

285 Oh, what a beautiful baby

You will need:

> Baby pictures of those taking part (plus any baby information about them from their relatives)
> Paper and pencils

Number the pictures and display them around the walls. Players try to guess whose pictures they are. They could also vote for the following:
1 The cutest baby
2 The funniest baby
3 The world's greatest burper
4 The most difficult baby
5 The noisiest baby
6 The most cuddly baby
7 The greatest guzzler
8 The most amusing baby

The climax of the game takes place when you ask the players, one by one, for their answers. You can 'work up' the party hilarity by displaying the titles on a board and then, one by one, asking the players to shout out their nominations.

The votes are counted and some small appropriate gift or symbol can be awarded, eg a dummy for the noisiest baby; a baby feeder for the greatest guzzler, and so on.

286 Parliamentary debate

team game

No equipment needed

Two teams face each other, while the chairman sits at the end between the two rows. The team leaders take turns to announce the motion which the house is going to debate. One team has to give reasons why they support the motion, while the other side gives reasons for opposing it as follows: the leader of team A announces the topic to be discussed and speaks in favour; the leader of team B speaks against the motion; the second member in team A gives a reason in favour; the second member of team B gives a reason against; and so on down the two rows.

To add to the fun, each member must stand up before speaking. Have humorous topics, eg 'all beards should be banned' or 'doughnuts are good for the waistline'. Appropriate 'boos', 'hear-hear' and all manner of calls will enliven the proceedings.

287 Penny waddle

You will need:

A small bowl
2p pieces

A small bowl is placed on the floor 3m from the starting line. Two players each place a coin between their knees, hold hands and waddle to the bowl, then try to drop the coin into it.

Played with two small teams this game has great spectator value.

288 Pin the tail on the Donkey

You will need:

A blindfold
A large picture of a donkey and a separate tail with pin/bluetack attached

Pin the picture of the donkey to the wall at a reachable height. One by one, blindfold the players and ask them to pin the tail in the appropriate place on the donkey. When they have had their turn, remove their blindfold and let them see where they have (often hilariously) positioned the tail. Make a small pencil mark on that spot. Blindfold each player in turn and ask them to pin the tail on the donkey. The winner is the player who manages to position the tail closest to where it should be.

289 Quaker's wedding

No equipment needed

Go round the players saying to each person:
'My friend Obadiah, the son of Zachariah, bids me to inquire of thee if thou wilt go with me to his wedding?'

The answer being 'yes', continue: 'Put thy finger to thy lips to keep thyself from laughing, and follow me.'

When all are following, with their fingers to their lips, perform various movements, which the others must imitate. Finally, kneel down on one knee, with everyone close beside you, in the same position. When all are quietly kneeling, suddenly lean sideways. The whole group will fall to the floor.

290 The peel

over-15s

You will need:

An apple and a knife for each contestant

This game should not be played with young children.

The object of the competition is to see who can peel the longest strip of peel from the apple within a given time limit.

291 Three minute time test

You will need:

A directions sheet for each player, as follows

Can you follow directions?
1. Read everything before doing anything.
2. Put your name in the upper right-hand corner of this paper.
3. Circle the 'name' in sentence two.
4. Draw five small squares in the upper left-hand corner of this paper.
5. Put an 'X' in each square.
6. Sign your name under the title of this paper.
7. Put a circle around sentence five.
8. Put an 'X' in the lower left-hand corner of this paper.
9. Draw a triangle around the 'X' you have just put down.
10. Draw a rectangle around the word 'paper' in sentence four.
11. Loudly call out your first name when you get to this point.
12. If you think you have followed the directions carefully to this point, call out, 'I have!'
13. On the reverse side of this paper, add up 8950 and 9850.
14. Put a circle around your answer and a square around the circle.
15. Count backwards in a normal speaking voice, from 10 to 1.
16. Punch three small holes in the top of this paper with your pencil point.
17. If you are first person to reach this point, call out loudly, 'I am the first person to reach this point, and I am the leader in following directions.'
18. Underline all the even numbers on this side of the paper.
19. Say out loudly, 'I am nearly finished and I have followed directions'.
20. Now that you have finished reading carefully, do only sentence two.

292 We want fireworks

all-age

You will need:

Balloons
Pins

A series of cards, each with one of the following titles, large enough for an audience to read easily.
1. AHH
2. WHISTLE
3. HOORAY
4. SHSHSHSH
5. CLAP
6. SSSSS
7. WE WANT FIREWORKS

The purpose of this game is to encourage audience participation. It is suitable for all ages, but particularly for children.

Hide some people outside the door or behind a screen/curtains, giving them the balloons and pins.

Show the cards one by one. The audience must do or say whatever is on them. Have a couple of trial runs. On the third round, the surprise ending occurs after they have cried out, 'We want fireworks!' Your hidden assistants burst the balloons with the pins. (In the open air, you could let off fireworks instead). The loud report ensures a good laugh.

10 Travel games

Travelling by road, train or car is a common experience in this mobile age. Traffic jams and congested roads often result in boredom and repetitious pleas from children 'How much further do we have to go?' Yet our journeys are good opportunities for 'looking' or observation games. The evergreen favourites like, 'I spy', 'Who am I' and 'First to see', will enliven many a trip and keep children amused. They can also enable the driver to concentrate without distraction.

Reading and writing games in a moving vehicle should be used sparingly – they may lead to travel sickness or eye strain. It is useful to have another adult as referee so that the driver is not too deeply involved. Set time limits at the beginning of games, or have a change of game every fifteen or twenty miles, depending on what you are playing. Don't forget to take along some boards or hardback books, for children to rest their paper on when games involve writing.

293 I spy

all-age

No equipment needed

A traditional favourite.

A child's power of observation can often surprise us, and they frequently have unusual ways at looking at objects and humans.

The first person to play looks around in the vehicle or outside, and chooses a suitable object visible to all. She says, 'I spy with my little eye something beginning with ...' and gives the initial letter of the object (eg if it was a lamp-post then it would be '... something beginning with L'). If the object is outside the vehicle, emphasise beforehand that it must be visible for the whole time – low-flying jet fighter planes will not do! All players call out what they think the letter stands for. The one who guesses correctly has the next turn. If the object has not been discovered after a short period (say 2 or 3 minutes), then the player posing the question has another turn.

An alternative question helpful for young children is, 'I spy with my little eye something the colour of...' (state a colour).

294 Car colour collection

No equipment needed

This is a useful game for a busy road when the journey is longer than half an hour.

Choose a car colour, eg 'red'. Players call out as soon as they see a red vehicle. The first to spot one scores one point. The first to have spotted twenty red cars is the winner, and the game can recommence. If two players call out together, no points are awarded. It is useful to have an adjudicator for this game!

295 Continuous Story

No equipment needed

This game is especially enjoyed by younger children.

Someone begins a story, 'Once upon a time...' then stops after two or three sentences. The next player continues the story for a few more sentences, and so on until all other occupants have made contributions. Finally, an adult concludes the story with a fantastic and thrilling end.

296 Name game

You will need:

Pencils and paper

Each player takes the first letter of his or her Christian or second name, and looks out for objects on the journey beginning with that same letter. The longest list after about fifteen minutes is the winner. This game can also be played by younger children, who call out objects they spot while an adult keeps the score.

297 Licence plate alphabet

You will need:

Alphabet sheets (see below)
Pencils

Write the letters of the alphabet down the left-hand side of the paper, or get the players to do this before they start. You will not need to include the letters I, O, Q and Z in the UK.

On the journey, look out for licence plate letters, trying to spot a car first with an 'A' on the plate, then 'B' and so on down the alphabet. A referee will definitely be needed to verify the claims! If no one can confirm the sighting, the claim is turned down.

298 It adds up to 50,000

You will need:

Pencils and paper or small calculators for each player

Players write down registration numbers they see, adding them up as they see them. The first person to score 50,000 or more is the winner.

299 Sing-a-long

No equipment needed

A player sings a nursery rhyme, the next sings a different one, and so on until everyone has sung something, one after another. But – here's the catch – once a song has been sung it cannot be repeated. Anyone singing a song which has already been sung is counted out. The game continues until no one can think of any more nursery rhymes.

300 Rhyme words

No equipment needed

The first player starts by saying, 'I know a word that rhymes with 'sink'. What is it?' The others have to guess what she has in mind. They may guess 'pink', 'link', 'stink', until they strike 'ink', – the word chosen by the first player. The player guessing the right word recommences the game. If a 'strike' is not made, the first player has another go.

301 Word search

'You will need:

Pencils and paper

For those who enjoy Scrabble-type games this can be fun on a journey. The adult player suggests a suitable word from which a number of smaller words can be made. The player with the longest list within a given time wins. For instance, the letters in the word 'Holiday' can make at least twenty words. If you are going on holiday, try words such as 'destination', 'travelling' or 'transport'.

302 Animal search

You will need:

Pencils and paper

This game is good for more rural journeys. Agree beforehand how many points are awarded for each animal spotted, eg a cat = 1 point, a rabbit = 20 points, a horse = 5 points. You could have a fruitful discussion with the children about the number of points awarded to each animal, and the reasons why. A consensus of views will save many an argument later!

Players take one side of the road or track as they search for animals. When they spot one, they write down its name and its worth in points. The first to score 100 points wins.

Index

Adapted hockey 7
Alphabet ping-pong ... 54
Altitude test 34
Americanisms 81
Animal search 95
Animals 34
Antiques and bygones 76
Apple bobbing 87
Are you... ? 54
Art gallery 55
Ascot bonnet 55
Associated numbers ... 55
Aunt Agatha's agony
    column 76
Autograph collecting . 77

Baby show 77
Back-to-back battle 8
Backside word shuffle 87
Ball catching 29
Balloon bursting 72
Balloon crackers 72
Balloon shavers 73
Balloon shower 73
Balloon smash 74
Balloon tossing 74
Balloon-bag burst 8
Balloons in the bucket 73
Balloons on the rails .. 73
Banana duel 8
Banana race 55
Battle ball 23
Beachcombers 35
Bean game 35
Beautiful Betsie Brown .. 87
Beetle 79
Big-bag ball escape 8
Bin-bag ball 74
Birthday cake 35
Bishop's riddle 77
Black and brown bears ... 35
Blast-off 9
Blind feeding 36
Blow line 36
Blowing in the wind .. 36
Boat race 37
Body charade 88
Body language 78
Book game 78
Book reviews 79
Bosses and secretaries 79
Bouncing ball 29
Bubbles 37
Bucket cricket 37
Building a pyramid 9

Camel race 26
Canopy volleyball 23
Capture the flag 10
Car colour collection . 94
Car names 80
Cards in bucket 37
Cat and mouse 23
Catching tails 29
Celebration census 89
Celebrity mix'n'match 38
Centipede shuffle 38
Changing places 55
Charades 56

Chinese laundry 56
Christmas introduction .
    80
Cinders' slipper 38
Circle pass out 10
Clang the bell 38
Climbing through
    newspaper 38
Collection relay 11
Continuous story 94
Contortions 39
Cops and robbers 11
Country quiz 81
County count 56
Crazy walks 88
Crocker 11
Cross-country
    motorama 26

Deer stalking 39
Defend the fort 40
Detection search 56
Dimensions 89
Discus throw 40
Dodge ball 12
Dog and bone 40
Don't kick the can 39
Double blow line 57
Downing doughnuts .. 40
Drawing clumps 81
Dressing race 41
Drink and blow 57
Duck fighting 57
Duster hockey 41

Easy! Easy! 41
Elastic bands 41
Electric fence 58
Escape ball 42
Exchange and credit .. 58

Falling dominoes 12
Farmyard frolic 42
Fashion parade 89
Feather football 58
Find the route 58
Fire! Fire! 12
Flapping the kipper ... 42
Follow the light 42
Food trivia 59
Foot word shuffle 89
Four-legged musical
    chairs 43
Front and back races . 43

Getting acquainted 59
Getting to know all
    about you 59
Getting to know you .. 60
Gladiators 43
Glove and hat race 44
Gossiping 60
Gourmet's relay 44
Grab a bag 44
Grab the loot 44
Grape toss 60
Group puzzles 44
Guess a weight! 89
Guess who! 45
Hand football 45
Hand wrestle 60

Handball 13
Handicap snatch 61
Happy families 61
Head of the river 61
Heads and tails 23
Here is the beehive 30
Here we come Loopy
    Loo 31
Here we go round the
    Mulberry bush 31
Hidden halves 45
Hockey, adapted 7
Hockey duster 41
Horsemen, knights and
    Henry VIII 62
How many beans? 45
Hugging honey 74
A human organ 86
Human noughts and
    crosses 62
Human obstacle course .
    46
Human scavenger hunt ..
    62
Human letters 46
Human spelling 62

I spy 93
I stamp my feet 31
If you're happy and you
    know it 30
Indian-file dodge ball 14
Informal skittle ball ... 14
Information collecting 15
Introductions 63
Inventions 82
Invisible make-up 90
It adds up to 50,000 ... 94

Jack Frost 39
Japanese wrestling
    scrum 63
Javelin throw 46
Jumbled names 82
Jump kangaroo 15

Kim's game 83
Knight's combat 63

Lace up 63
Last chance 90
Learning DIY 63
Let's pretend 31
Licence plate alphabet 94
Long John stuff 64

Magic ball 32
Making a tent 23
Milko 64
Mime rhyme 64
Miming game 64
Miss Polly had a dolly 31
Moustache 46
Mushroom 24
Musical bizarre poses 46
Musical bumps 31
Musical chaos 47
Musical couples 47
Musical laps 64
Musical mats 47

Name game 94
Nature trail 15
Nehemiah's wall 15
Numbers game 83

Obstacle race 27
Oh, what a beautiful
    baby 90
On target 65
One minute, please ... 65
Open, shut them 32

Paper ball fight 47
Paper delivery 65
Parliamentary debate . 90
Pass the key 65
Passing the coins 47
Passing the Polo 66
The peel 91
Peg a person 66
Penny waddle 91
Phobias 83
Pick-up sticks 15
Pictures and puzzles .. 47
Pig to market 48
Pigeon and eagle 48
Piggyback jousting 16
Pin the tail on the
    donkey 91
Pinball soccer 66
Plank race 17
Pop goes the weasel ... 32
Portraits 84
Posing 48
Press-gang chain 17
Punch ball 24
Push ball 27

Quaker's wedding 91
Quiet please 30

Random handball 17
Rhyme words 95
Rhythm band 48
Ring a ring o'roses 32
Roll up 49
Roller coaster 24
Romantic letters 66
Rounders 17
Rugby scrum 28

Sale bargains 49
Scavenger hunt 18
The sea and her
    children 51
Sea battle 16
Serious laughter 68
Shipwreck 49
Shoe kicking 67
Shoe scramble 24
Shoe shucking 67
Shopping 49
Shunting tunnel 18
Sign up 84
Signatures 84
Silent Christmas
    menu 85
Simon says 16
Sing-a-long 94
Skittle ball 50
Small box stack 49

Smells galore 85
Soccer slalom 18
Sock it 67
Sock shop 67
Spacemen 74
Spaceship 19
Speedway 49
Spinning the hoop 32
Squirrels 32
Stand up! 19
Stations 32
Story mime 50
Story time 50
Storytelling 24
Sumo wrestling 50
Swap 25

Tagging the team 51
Team refreshments ... 67
Tent-making 23
The farmer's in his
    den 30
Three back race 68
Three-minute time test .
    92
Three-legged fun 19
Tightrope test 68
Tipping the waste 68
Tissue whirlwind 51
Title miming 69
Toeing 51
Toilet roll capers 69
Tommy Thumb 33
Topple the king 52
Train 33
Tramps' tea party 52
Treasure chest 52
Tree game 85
Trussing 69
Tube stations 69
Tunnel relay 28
Turtle 25
Tutti-frutti 52
Twenty questions 70
Twin tug of war 19
The two hats 68

Uncrowning the
    monarch 53

Vacancy! 70
Volleyball (a simple
    version) 20

Walk the line 71
Water wide game 21
We want fireworks 92
Welly throwing 28
What a character 71
What a surprise! 71
What's the time
    Mr Wolf? 33
Wheelbarrow
    marathon 21
Wheelbarrow race 28
Wink and run 70
Word search 95
Wrapping the team ... 53